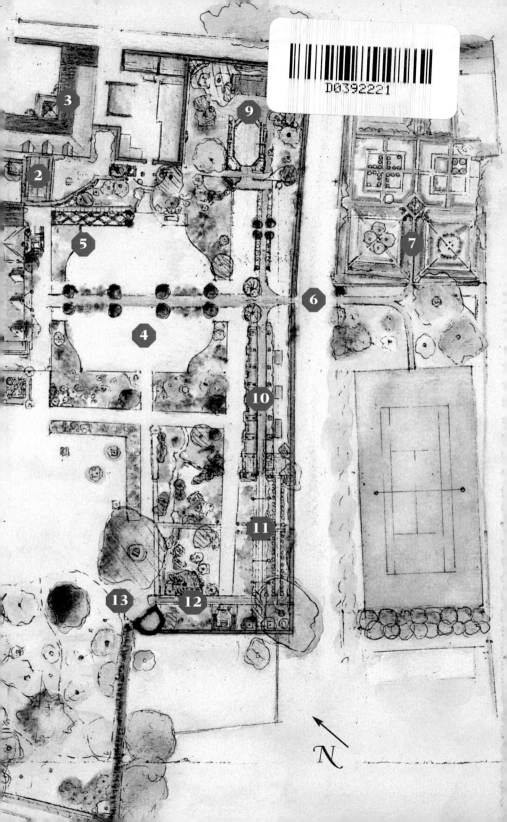

N

Rosemary Verey

Rosemary Verey

THE LIFE & LESSONS OF A
LEGENDARY GARDENER

BY

Barbara Paul Robinson

DAVID R. GODINE
Publisher · Boston

To my husband, Charles Raskob Robinson,
my partner in our garden,
and to our sons, Charles and Torrance,
who as young boys both worked so hard in it.

———————

First published in 2012 by
DAVID R. GODINE · *Publisher*
Post Office Box 450
Jaffrey, New Hampshire 03452
www.godine.com

LIBRARY OF CONGRESS
CATALOGING-IN-PUBLICATION DATA

Robinson, Barbara Paul.
Rosemary Verey : the life & lessons of a
legendary gardener / by Barbara Paul Robinson.
p. cm.
ISBN 978-1-56792-450-3 – ISBN 1-56792-450-6
1. Verey, Rosemary. 2. Gardeners—England—Biography.
3. Gardens—Design. I. Title.
SB63.V37R63 2012
635.092´241–dc23
2011053541

Second Printing, 2013
PRINTED IN THE UNITED STATES

CONTENTS

I feel so fortunate to have known dear Rosemary. And it was a lucky turn of fate that I moved to Gloucestershire twenty-four years ago and found that one of its treasures lived not far down the road. As a result I was able to pick the determined brain of a true plantswoman to the everlasting benefit of Highgrove. The true value of her contribution is contained in the voluminous correspondence I have stored away in my archives in which she transmitted endless advice and suggestions, interspersed with her inimitable enthusiasm and affection.

It all seems so strange without her now, but there are corners of my garden which will be "forever Rosemary" and an abiding impression I have of her to this day is of her climbing out of the cockpit of a very small aeroplane for her eightieth birthday – dashing, determined, incorrigible and loving as ever.

With permission of His Royal Highness The Prince of Wales
reprinted from "Remembrances of Rosemary,"
a privately issued booklet compiled by Katherine Lambert,
April 25, 2004.

Rosemary Verey

My Boss, My Mentor, My Friend

 OSEMARY VEREY was my boss, and later she became my teacher, my mentor, and my special friend. My husband, Charlie, will tell you that she changed my life. I went to work for her in her famous garden at Barnsley House, in Gloucestershire, England, in the spring of 1991 when she was seventy-two years old and at the height of her powers. She came to gardening late in her life, a self-taught amateur who became internationally renowned as a garden designer, plantswoman, and writer. By the time I met her she was the "must have" garden designer for the rich and famous, not only in England, but around the world. Her clients included Prince Charles and Elton John. Even the Japanese, with their distinct gardening aesthetic, enlisted her to design an English-style garden for the Hankyu Department Store in Osaka. Her own beautiful garden, Barnsley, in the heart of the Cotswolds, was a mandatory stop on every garden tourist's itinerary. More than 30,000 visitors per year came by the busloads from as far away as Japan and Australia. She was particularly popular in America where an interest in gardening was burgeoning. Appreciative audiences flocked to her lectures, and her eighteen books were best-sellers, especially in the States.

The moment was right for Rosemary to revive the English

romantic style after decades of deprivation following the two world wars. Economic hardship and lack of skilled gardening labor led to what some would describe as the nadir of British gardening, with its emphasis on low maintenance ground covers. Instead, using her garden as her classroom, she re-introduced classical garden designs, favoring formal structures, planting knot gardens and using hedges and box balls. Being a superb plantswoman, she embellished formal outlines with exuberant flower borders maintained to perfection, creating beautiful pictures by using harmonious color combinations and a mix of textures. Her famous potager was based on the grand gardens at Villandry, France, but she scaled the ideas down to a smaller, workable scale. She broke new ground in England and America by mixing flowers and vegetables together, planted in complex patterns intended to be both productive and visually appealing.

She was at heart a teacher and an effective communicator, sharing her enthusiasm and the knowledge she had gained from hands-on experience in creating her own garden at Barnsley. Always learning herself, she was open to new ideas and enjoyed her interactions with people. Her writing and her lectures were more like conversations than sermons. She believed any garden should relate well to the house and its environs, a lesson that now seems obvious but had been forgotten. And because Barnsley itself was relatively small, less than four acres, she made beautiful gardens seem possible to the average homeowner. Her message was that you, too, could do this if you tried.

How did this English lady gardener become such a horticultural icon? And what was it that made her particularly successful in America? Although I came to know her very well, I wanted to better understand how she had managed to become world famous when it seemed much more likely that she would live out her life much like countless English country ladies with a nice house, a respectable family, and an attractive garden. As I faced my own senior years, I was intrigued by the fact she began her career after her children had grown. She first took to gardening in her forties and published her first book when she was sixty-two, an age when most people expect to slow down and plan to retire.

My connection to Rosemary began on a cold day in March in New York City. I can still vividly recall walking across Central Park to be interviewed by her. I was very nervous, intent on persuading her to allow me to come work for her in her garden. I hoped my fingernails didn't look too manicured and tried to settle the butterflies in my stomach. I wasn't quite sure what to expect or how to behave. For the past twenty-five years, I had been practicing law in New York City at Debevoise & Plimpton, first as a young associate fresh out of Yale Law School and then as the firm's first female partner. I had earned a once-in-a-lifetime sabbatical, a precious chance to break away from my pressured professional life.

My own evolving gardening passion had led to this moment. More than twenty years before Charlie, and I bought an old wreck of an eighteenth-century farmhouse in northwestern Connecticut as a weekend retreat for ourselves and our two young sons. In the process of restoring the house and clearing the land, I had slowly succumbed to a passion for plants. Like Rosemary, I was self taught but hungry to learn more. When I failed to find the perfect course to fit into the short time frame of my sabbatical, a friend suggested I try to work in a great garden instead. I grabbed the idea and wrote somewhat audaciously to two of the most famous English women gardener-writers, Rosemary Verey and Penelope Hobhouse, asking if I might come work as one of their gardeners without pay. To be certain that they would take my request seriously, I asked gardening friends who knew them to write and vouch for me, to verify that I wouldn't be a danger in their gardens and more important, to say that I wouldn't be a pain in the neck.

In response to my letter, Rosemary Verey called me, her voice rather crisp and impersonal. She said she couldn't agree to my proposal without meeting me first, but added, "I am coming to New York in early March for the New York Flower Show. Why don't I come to your office on my way into town from the airport for a brief interview?" I hadn't been interviewed in over twenty-five years; I normally do the interviewing, mostly young law students seeking to work in my firm. Afraid that my imposing corner office in midtown Manhattan would send the wrong message and suggest that I'd expect to be pampered, treated like a guest, unwilling to work hard and learn, I replied, "Why don't I come to see you wherever you're staying after you've had a chance to freshen up?" Then the day arrived and I was heading off to someone's Fifth Avenue apartment with sweaty palms, wondering what the famous Mrs. Verey would decide. I desperately wanted her to like me enough to say yes.

When she opened the door, she looked smaller than I expected. Her white hair was carefully coifed, her light blue eyes behind her glasses sharply sized me up, her smile was pleasant but formal. She was wearing her signature multi-stranded pearls, a long, loose skirt, a crisp blouse, and a colorfully embroidered wool jacket with sensible flat shoes. Her host had already left for work so we had the place to ourselves. As we went into the kitchen for a cup of tea, she helped me relax by talking about what was happening at Barnsley this time of year. But I could tell she was also testing my plant knowledge without being too obvious about it.

After awhile, we moved into the antique-cluttered living

room after passing through a surprising dining room adorned with large cages full of live birds. We both wondered what it would be like to dine there amidst the cacophony and flying feathers. I was pleased to see she had a sense of humor. Then she began to ask me pointed questions. "Will you need to use the garden truck? The last American girl who worked for me abused that privilege and we need the truck for the garden." I promised I would rent a car. Then, after offering me the free use of the gardener's cottage, she asked, "Are you prepared to pay for the utilities?" "But of course," I replied. She warned me that the cottage was small, and I would have to look after myself. Finally, with a penetrating look, she described her two gardeners as "working-class boys" who hadn't finished high school, then asked the key question, "Are you prepared to be treated like staff?" With her English accent, the last word came out elongated, sounding like "s-t-a-a-a-a-a-h-f."

I knew exactly what she meant and was relieved I hadn't allowed her to come to my office. It was clear that she would be my boss. Instead of answering directly, I asked whether her gardeners were knowledgeable. She replied, "Of course. They have worked for me for years, and I have taught them everything they know." Finally, I asked whether they would mind working with me. She pondered for a moment and then said with a smile, "I shouldn't think so. They will probably just be quite amused." Then it was done; I was "hired." She indicated the date of my arrival in late April in her diary, writing in her signature green ink. I was elated.

One of the delightful discoveries I made while pursuing the research for this book was the diary entry I found in her papers for the day of my interview. My name was entered next to the time scheduled as "Barbara Robinson (Robertson?)." Then, always astute about people, she later added

Introduction

"Barbara Robinson came to see me re coming to work at BH for one month this summer. Do hope it's not mad of me to take her on!"

One month later, I drove my small rental car from London on the two-hour trip west to Barnsley on the wrong side of the road. I kept repeating to myself, "Think left, think left!" Driving through the soft, rolling green hills of the Cotswolds, the velvet fields dotted with cows and sheep, outlined by golden limestone walls, I noticed the landscape seemed greener, gentler, and more continuously cultivated than my Litchfield County hills. In early April, the fresh chartreuse of emerging foliage dusted everything, spring flowers appeared in the verges, and masses of white blossoms adorned the hedgerows along the small roads. The very trees seemed to stand grander and more majestic than anything in Connecticut.

I arrived on a Saturday and drove up the driveway, through handsome iron gates set in tall stone walls into the adjacent parking field already full of cars and buses delivering visitors to the garden. A sign read, "Please Park Tidily." Rosemary was there, deeply engaged, signing her books and selling plants, leading groups through the garden while answering questions and recounting the history of Barnsley House. After a cursory greeting from my "boss," I was sent off to find my cottage in the company of Margie, another new gardener who would become my daily pal.

My small, spartan stone cottage faced the main road running through the village of Barnsley, at the end of a row of three attached cottages that housed Rosemary's gardeners. After settling in, I drove the four miles to the nearest large town of Cirencester to stock up on food and supplies, then returned to find Rosemary (then Mrs. Verey to me) alone in the garden, counting the money after the visitors had left and the garden was closed. The rest of the staff had fled shortly before for their day off. I was thrilled to have Mrs. V. and the garden all to myself. We sat opposite each other over a table in the potting shed, where I would spend many hours in the weeks to come, potting up, pricking out, striking cuttings, selling books and plants, collecting the money. Open to the air on one side, the shed was part of an enclosed sales yard lined by small greenhouses around outdoor tables full of plant offerings. Against the back wall of the shed hung a pegboard, cleverly painted with the outlines of each hand tool, showing exactly where they belonged. I noticed that the staff had not completely complied when they put their tools back, but it seemed a brilliant idea nonetheless.

I was about to receive my first lesson. Rosemary showed me the proper way to fold the paper money and to roll the coins, explaining that her system made it easier at the bank. A simple matter but a clear indication that there was going to be a proper way to do things and it would be the Rosemary Verey way. I could tell she would be a strict taskmaster, a tough and demanding boss, but one who enjoyed the teaching role.

On Monday, I started work promptly at 8:00 A.M. trying to ignore the cold drizzle. Mrs. V. was not yet out, but I met the "boys," Andy and Les Bailey, the brothers who had worked there for more than fourteen years. These two immediately began their daily routines, but first set me to work. Andy explained that the first chore of each day was the "dead-'eading." Handing me a bucket and "secateurs" ("clippers" to me), Andy sent me out to dead-head the spent flowers in the garden to make it presentable for the public. Clumsy in my rain gear, I was too terrified to step right into the deep, lush flower borders to snip off the head of some wilted daffodil or tulip, sure I would trample too many treasures, or, worse, that I would fall, crushing all the plants beneath me. When I returned empty handed, Andy said simply, "Well, you can't make an omelet without breaking a few eggs."

When Mrs. V. arrived shortly thereafter, we all snapped to attention. Then Andy and Les fell into line behind her to walk through the garden, as she, clipboard in hand, pointed at things to be done, jotting each down on a list. Her white hair uncovered, she stood straight and undaunted in the cold rain. This trio had been together for so long that not many words were needed. Just some pointing and mumbling, with several stops and pauses, punctuated by a few "umms" or "aahs." While the boys did not audibly sigh with relief when Mrs. V. went back inside the house, their mood definitely lightened.

Only a few days after I arrived, Mrs. V. departed for Michigan where she was designing a garden, leaving the staff in charge. Although I was disappointed by her absence, the others clearly relished their freedom. When Mrs. V. returned, we were subjected to what felt like a military inspection. Pots of small plants were picked up, weighed in her hand and found to be too light. Clearly they needed water. How had we failed to notice? The watering cans were judged to hold water we hadn't warmed sufficiently for the tender seedlings. The compost was not in the potting shed, things were untidy and the garden badly in need of attention. We all fell in, set to, quickened our pace, and followed her orders.

I worked at Barnsley House for a month; it was an intense and marvelous experience. In the following decade of her life, I stayed with Rosemary at Barnsley whenever I could and she often came to stay with me either in New York City or in Connecticut on her many trips to America. I called her virtually every Sunday for the rest of her life. One of my favorite memories took place during one visit to Barnsley that Rosemary and Charlie arranged to get me started on writing a book about my garden. Rosemary decreed that I would stay indoors to write every morning until lunch before she allowed me to go out to play. One night when I was fast asleep, I awoke to noises outside my bedroom window. I got up to see what was going on. It was three o'clock in the morning, but in the darkness below I could see it was Rosemary. Her white hair glowed in the moonlight as she moved through the garden dressed only in her cotton nightie. It had been a dry summer and she was moving the sprinklers to be sure to water all the lawns. I wanted to grow up to be just like her.

Rosemary taught me important lessons about gardening, but she also taught me more profound lessons about life. Just like all good lessons, they are simple and clear. And once learned, seem obvious but not easy to put into practice. By her own example, her most essential lessons were about character and discipline. About setting high standards, about stamina, energy, and drive. One of the most important lessons I learned from Rosemary was to take risks, to "just get on with it."

Having lived and worked at Barnsley, I also saw another darker side of Rosemary, one she concealed from her public. After the death of her husband, she was often home alone. In her solitude, she began to drink too much. It may have been the drinking that caused her unpredictable eruptions that seared close friendships and tested those around her. Like many strong-willed, successful people, she could be difficult, demanding, and complicated. Self-disciplined and a striver for perfection, Rosemary drove herself as hard as she drove those who worked for her. And, as is often the case, she could be hardest on those closest to her. Whatever the reason for her drinking and her outbursts, Rosemary was a product of her times and upbringing. She did not discuss her emotions or indulge in self-reflection. At heart, those who knew her best sensed a deep insecurity, a need to feel loved.

If Rosemary had been born in a later era, she would have likely succeeded in something other than gardening, possibly one of the professions or even politics. Highly intelligent and extremely hard working, she also loved an audience and audiences in turn loved her, thanks to her special flare, great charm, and sense of fun. She was vibrant, engaging, the life of any party. Even before the word had been invented, she was the ultimate networker, a shameless self-promoter who delighted in being the center of attention. But she was constrained by her time and the conventional expectations of English women of her upper social class. Gardening was a suitable arena for someone of her background, and she made the most of it. She followed a long line of English lady gardeners and writers, such as Gertrude Jekyll, Norah Lindsay, Margery Fish, and Vita Sackville-West.

Her eventual success was in part due to luck and timing, but Rosemary certainly seized the moment. After the two world wars, many of the magnificent gardens of the great English estates had been turned into lawn as cheap gardening labor disappeared into the factories. By the 1970s, the economy began to recover and conditions were ripe for Rosemary to re-introduce the English to their own garden heritage and traditions. In America, home ownership had grown along with the expanding suburbs, and Americans were traveling to Europe in growing numbers as flights became easier and more affordable, developing more sophisticated tastes for European styles in food, furnishing, and gardens.

The public was ready for Rosemary's message that anyone could have a beautiful garden and could do it themselves, just as she had. Through her lectures, articles, and eighteen books, she taught lessons about plant combinations and the importance of structure, color, texture, and appealing to all the senses. She wrote in clear, lucid prose that was neither too poetic nor too erudite, offering know-how and practical advice while urging her audience to express themselves. With real insight, someone called her the "great encourager."

Gardens are ephemeral. Rosemary's gardens at Barnsley House continue to be maintained by a fancy hotel that has taken over, but they are not the same. Her eye and hand have gone, but Rosemary's legacy will endure through her books and her influence on those who will always love beautiful gardens. For those lucky enough to have known her, Rosemary will also be remembered for her indomitable spirit. She was great fun. Her favorite saying was, "It's a sin to be dull." And she never was.

CHAPTER ONE

'Early Years and Marriage
1918–1939

*My family did not allow me
to be seriously competitive.*

N A COLD, wet day in December 1998, a small plane painted in crisp red, white, and blue with a black-and-white striped single-propeller circles the Royal Flying Corps Rendcomb Airfield awaiting the arrival of H.R.H. The Prince of Wales below. Rosemary Verey, the internationally renowned plantswoman, writer, and garden designer, sits freezing and impatient in the open cockpit. She knows that over sixty of her friends have come from near and as far away as America; they are waiting for her to arrive to celebrate her eightieth birthday. Because protocol normally requires royalty to arrive last, it is a great tribute to Rosemary that the Prince has arranged to arrive before she does to greet her. But there is still no sign of the Prince.

Rosemary asks the pilot, her friend and neighbor, Vic Norman, "Can't we do a loop-de-loop so I can keep warm?" Besides it would be such fun! She knows, because she has done the loop-de-loop with him before. Vic is relieved he can skip it this time when he finally sees the Prince's car arriving on the field. Instead of performing the loop-de-loop, he circles once more so Rosemary can wave to the assembled crowd below before he lands. Beautifully dressed in a flaming red suit and purple scarf designed by her friend, Sir Hardy Amies, designer to the Queen, she is helped out of the cockpit onto the wing, her hair a bit windblown but not nearly as mussed as it would have been after a loop-de-loop. She alights from the plane beaming into Prince Charles's open arms.[1]

The Prince stays on for half an hour or so talking with the guests, then leaves so the party can continue without his intimidating presence. Inside an old engine shed, Rupert Golby, one of Rosemary's former gardeners who has gone on to his own success as a garden designer, has decorated the interior to evoke a charming potting shed. Antique watering cans filled with rich red amaryllis, bouquets of red anemones and blue iris, balls of garden twine, boxwood topiary, and apple tree branches adorn the tables covered with red-and-white checkered tablecloths, flanked by red cloth folding chairs. Each place has a small flower pot containing a napkin and sprig of rosemary. Scenes from Rosemary's own famous gardens at Barnsley House hang on the walls. Rosemary always loves a good party and this is just one of several that will follow in other venues to celebrate her eightieth birthday.

For all her fame around the world, Rosemary certainly cherished most her work for Prince Charles and their special friendship. In his foreword in a memorial booklet after her death in 2001, Prince Charles wrote, "I feel so fortunate to have known dear Rosemary. It was a lucky turn of fate that I moved to Gloucestershire . . . and found that one of its treasures lived not far down the road. As a result, I was able to pick the determined brain of a true plantswoman. . . . She transmitted endless advice and suggestions, interspersed with her inimitable enthusiasm and affection. There are corners of my garden which will be "forever Rosemary" and an abiding impression I have of her to this day is of her climbing out of the cockpit of a very small aeroplane for her eightieth birthday – dashing, determined, incorrigible, and loving as ever."[2]

Rosemary was born on the winter solstice, December 21, 1918, just after the close of the First World War to a respectable upper middle class English family. But for her arrival on a propitious date, it would have been hard to predict the arc of a life that would bring her to worldwide fame. It seemed much more likely that she would grow up to live her life as one of countless anonymous conventional country ladies with a nice house and garden, who devoted herself to raising her family and supporting her church. Yet when Rosemary died in 2001, lengthy obituaries paying her tribute appeared in all the major newspapers, including the *Times* of London and the *New York Times*, as well as a full page in the less than horticulturally inclined *Economist*. Some speculated her birth on the winter solstice was prophetic; the stars would align for the rest of her life.

When Rosemary arrived, the war to end all wars had just ended. The English way of life had already begun to change as the gentry learned to make do without the servants lost to the war effort and England began recovering from the devastating loss of a generation of young men. The flu pandemic was also taking its toll on the population, with more than one hundred million deaths around the world. Born into a military family, Rosemary Isabel Baird Sandilands was the youngest of four children of Prescott Sandilands, an officer in the Royal Marines, and Gladys Murton, a former actress nicknamed "Slugs." The pampered baby of the family, Rosemary joined the company of her older brother, Pat, named for her father, who was seven years older; Francis, who arrived two years after Pat; and her sister Christina, born a year after that. The gap of four years before Rosemary arrived was due, one would guess, to the intervening war years.

Rosemary adored her father and often talked of him later in her life. Prescott Sandilands was handsome and charming, but not very practical. His military salary was barely sufficient to raise and educate his four children in a style deemed appropriate to their social class. Finances were stretched, but Rosemary's mother, a strong and intelligent woman, somehow managed it all even though the family was always short of money. Her friend and eventual sister-in-law, Gillian Lady Sandilands, observed that she "brought up all those children, found them all places at school. She was marvelous with them and she was very bright. I think that is where Rosemary gets her brains from."

In many ways, Rosemary took after her actress-mother, inheriting her quick intelligence and her striking ice-blue eyes. Although she rarely talked much about her mother or their relationship, later in her life she did contrast her mother with her father. "My father had impeccable manners, but he wasn't a great do'er. My mother was a great do'er.... My mother was a great influence on me."[3] Rosemary would certainly prove to be a "do'er."

More often it was her father she recalled. But then Rosemary would always prefer the company of men. Her father must have cut quite a dashing figure in his officer's uniform, and Rosemary was clearly proud of him. Military life caused the Sandilands family to move around, so Rosemary spent her early childhood familiar with various Royal Marine barracks. She said, "I have vivid memories of the band practicing on the parade grounds. Every time I hear a military band, I feel they're playing for me."[4] Something akin to her father's military discipline would be a fundamental trait of Rosemary's adult character.

When she was ten, her father retired from the Royal Marines with the rank of Lieutenant-Colonel. He settled the family down in the North of England at Nortoft House, in Guilsborough, Northamptonshire. Life changed dramatically for the young Rosemary, especially when she graduated from her bicycle to her first pony. Horses would become a passion for the rest of her life; she would grow into a skilled and fearless rider and a devoted member of the local hunt.

Shortly after the move to Northamptonshire, Rosemary and her sister were sent away to board at Eversley School in Folkestone, Kent, where they qualified for scholarship aid; it helped that their mother and aunt had gone there in the 1890s. Pat, the eldest son, embarked on a military career like his father and also qualified for financial support for his education at Willington. Francis, the second son, was the beneficiary of the generosity of an aunt who paid for his tuition at Eton as her own son, who had intended to go there, had died tragically young.

Rosemary spent nine years at the Eversley School and admitted that she had almost no interest in gardening. The school was very traditional. All the girls wore uniforms with white crisp collars and striped ties. Visiting ladies came properly attired in hats and gloves. There, she was "trained not to waste good time. There was this amazing feeling of discipline and we didn't fight it. It was part of life."[5]

Rosemary devoted her energies to her schoolwork and athletics. "I loved playing games – tennis, lacrosse, netball, even ping-pong – which I regarded as a due reward after geography and science lessons."[6] Her competitive spirit was already apparent. By twelve, she had won a pony competition, and at sixteen, she won the Kent County Girls Single Championship in tennis. A year later, she lost in the finals due to "too much partying. My family did not allow me to be seriously competitive, but it was fun, and a great honour later to be allowed to play for the county."

Despite her competitive nature and drive, Rosemary would always remain a product of the conventions and expectations of her generation and class. In her school years, she did not start out following the most predictable path for a young woman. Instead, her "one ambition was to go to college and study mathematics, the subject I most enjoyed," an area of study by no means an easy or obvious choice for women. At that time, very few women would have even thought of seeking a college degree. But Rosemary was a bright student and her record was sufficiently impressive to cause the head-mistress to be "generous" and send her "weekly to a tutor at Southampton University, who taught me enough to get me a place at University College, London."[7]

In 1937, Rosemary enrolled at University College and moved in with her parents who had left Northamptonshire to take up residence at Coleherne Court on the Old Brompton Road in London. Instead of math, she found herself more interested in history and switched to economics and social history. Although economics was an unlikely subject for a woman, it is hard to know why she abandoned mathematics, the subject she most enjoyed and would later credit for her interest in garden design patterns. Her tutor was Hugh Gaitskell who was then lecturing there. Gaitskell would go on to lead the Labour Party in England for many years and become a forceful member of Parliament. Although he was highly regarded and was a contender, he never did become Prime Minister. Still, he must have been an exciting mentor and demanding tutor. It was an interesting time to study economics, with the world just beginning to emerge from the Great Depression. Hitler was on the rise and England's leaders were intent on avoiding another war. In that same year, the King abdicated his throne to become the Duke of Windsor and marry Wallis Simpson; King George VI and his wife Queen Elizabeth were crowned.

Despite the tensions in Europe and the threat of war, life in London for those in the right circles continued predictably, observing longstanding social traditions. During the months of May, June, and July, a period that is still referred to as the "London Season," the major social events take place since there are better odds that the weather will cooperate, at least some of the time. Ascot, Wimbledon, and the British Open all take place in June. For a girl her age, Rosemary was expected to be presented to society as a debutante and attend the endless rounds of parties and balls.

Thus began Rosemary's schizophrenic existence; her serious academic studies were "in complete contrast to my debbing season and all the dances I went to in London and the country. It was like living in two quite different worlds."[8] Rosemary's life as a debutante was almost a full-time job, yet somehow she managed to juggle her social whirl with her studies. Before the phrase was invented, she was a successful "multitasker."

Suitable young men were enlisted to serve as escorts for the debutantes. David Farquharson, who was chosen for Rosemary, recalls her radiating energy and fun. She was "good value . . . full of life, always bursting with energy, and quite fearless too. I got asked to a certain number of deb dances – all the debutantes scrounge around all the boyfriends they know and ask them to come as their partners. I found out I was to escort Rosemary. Apparently it was her first deb dance." The "routine generally was that one would meet one's partner about 7 P.M. or so and go and have cocktails and dinner and then the ball wouldn't start until 10 or half past. Then you would go on to the ball and then at about 2 there'd be supper – the band played until about 3 or 4 in the morning and you'd finish up with bacon and eggs."

We "always had a jolly good laugh together and I think she had a great sense of humor. " David, himself a champion diver, remembers inviting Rosemary for a visit to his family's country house that year. When they went swimming, David displayed his prowess by performing a rather daring dive. "I won the diving at Eton and I learned to do some fancy diving – I was good enough to compete in the Canadian springboard diving championship. I did a 1½ somersault dive off the spring board in this lake so Rosemary said she'd try it. It's not the kind of dive one takes lightly. [She did] the most awful belly flop but she came out laughing." This was an early example of her competitive nature and willingness to take risks. David found her "a lot of fun, because she played tennis, she'd ride, she'd swim – she wasn't all that sexy and attractive but she wasn't unsexy either. She wasn't particularly beautiful, but very good company, very cheerful company, very nice smile; she'd laugh like hell at everything."

That energy, fearlessness, and sense of fun attracted many young men. Her girlfriend, Gillian Jackson, who would become Gillian Sandilands when she married Rosemary's favorite brother, Francis, confirmed that Rosemary had "lots of suitors, but none of them were particularly suitable, none were intellectual." Rosemary set off with one such unsuitable young man on a daring adventure. His father owned a sporting goods shop, which gave him access to every kind of sporting equipment. After outfitting the two of them with water skis, they skied down the Thames, dodging their way through the barges and other heavy water traffic, zooming under London's bridges. It must have been terribly dangerous. The Thames was a major thoroughfare, the equivalent of the modern highway, full of traffic, as well as pollution.

What a sight they must have been, those two young people on skis, racing through the watery heart of London!

During the deb parties, Rosemary danced with David Verey for the first time. They had known each other for many years since David was a close friend and Eton schoolmate of her brother, Francis. David had often visited the Sandilands family but there was a five-year age gap between David and Rosemary. Before her coming out, Rosemary was the little kid sister, and David must have seemed distant and far too old to incite any romantic interest. They had paid very little attention to each other before that fateful dance. Rosemary discovered "he was the best waltzer." He was also quiet, intellectual, and far more respectable than the likes of her waterskiing friend.

David Verey was the only child of Cecil Verey, a parson, and his wife, Constance Lindoraii Verey. The Vereys were an "aristocratic parsonage family. They were all vicars and rectors and they'd been sort of writers and dilettantes – perfect dilettantes."[9] David was not only the single child of his parents, but also the sole descendant of most of his uncles and aunts. By contrast, Rosemary's lineage included a solid banking family, although she often boasted about a more distinguished ancestor, claiming to be a descendant of Eleanor of Aquitaine, Queen of Henry II, pointing out the "heart on the Coat of Arms of the Sandilands came from the twelfth century." That coat of arms would later hang in her guest powder room. "Typical play it down Brit – but make sure everybody sees it!"[10]

David Verey had finished reading architecture at Trinity College, Cambridge, and had joined the Royal Fusiliers. Notwithstanding his military enlistment, he still had time to participate in the 1939 London season and enjoy that waltz Rosemary recalled. There is nothing in David's diaries to suggest he particularly noticed her or that dance. Instead, his diary recorded dancing until 2:30 A.M. with another young woman named Barbara Russell after he took her to the ballet. "It was the greatest fun. I think I've 'got it' worse than ever before." His diary is full of references to Barbara; but by March of 1939, he wrote that the relationship proved to be "a little hell as it is not reciprocated. All rather pathetic." He shared his disappointment with his mother, noting that "owing to some instinct of self-preservation I had not gone right off the deep end. And last night was in the nick of time; but it is very unpleasant all the same."[11]

The threat of another war provided a sobering backdrop to that social season. David worried about Chamberlain as "the only string on which peace is hung . . . if Chamberlain goes what will happen?" On April 8: "Mussolini chose yesterday to bomb the defenseless towns of her friendly little neighbor Albania. The British press is indignant in these terms at the sudden Italian conquest. . . . It is a world shock." He listened to Hitler's infamous Reichstag speech on the afternoon of April 28 and drew upon his religious convictions for strength. A few months earlier, David noted that a relative, Philip Verey had a son, the "first Verey birth since mine." But days later, there is a sad note that the little boy died. David continued to be the sole male descendant carrying the Verey family name.

As David worried about the threat of war and the "world going from crisis and making everything uncertain," he learned that after several attempts he had failed to pass parts of the exams required for licensed architects. At one point, after losing his job with an architectural firm, he almost gave up in frustration. "I have decided not to go on with architecture."[12]

That summer, David was asked to escort a group of school boys on a trip to Canada, but didn't want to leave his mother who had suffered a fall while moving into Barnsley House with her husband. Then he changed his mind, observing, "It's my well-known weakness in character to feel compelled to change after a decision has been made." Before he left, Rosemary's brother and David's close friend, Francis Sandilands, announced his engagement to Gill Jackson. To celebrate and bid David good-bye, the newly engaged couple and Rosemary paid a visit to Barnsley. They all enjoyed lots of tennis. David thought "Rosemary . . . did not need much entertaining as she fitted in very well in my family life. . . . I think I could know her much better now Francis is engaged and so engaged."[13]

After David sailed away in August on the Cunard White Star Liner SS *Andania* with the group of boys for a three-week tour of Canada, the situation in Europe deteriorated. At the end of the long crossing, he learned of the Soviet–German non-aggression pact, which "appeared at once as a terrible setback to the peace front." A few days later, David received a telegram instructing him that "his duty was to remain with the boys and not return to England owing to the crisis . . . an awful day of anxiety. There seems no hope."[14] That September, instead of returning to the horrors of war at home, several of the boys were relocated to schools and universities in Canada. On September 1, David wrote, "The war has apparently begun today. A day of very mixed emotions. Profoundly depressed at times. Also incredulous. We cannot realize here [in Canada] what the atmosphere in England must be like today when Hitler has actually attacked Poland."

After his month away, David sailed home that September. On the way back, his ship went off course to rescue the crew of a torpedoed British vessel. At home in Barnsley, he mused upon the Devil and why God did not prevent war before noting in a perfunctory way that he "wrote and proposed to

Rosemary."[15] He sent a telegram that was "terse and unromantic." It asked, "Will you marry me?"[16]

Two weeks later, David went to meet Rosemary at Kings Cross station on her return from Edinburgh. After a dinner, he drove her home and wrote simply, "We are engaged."[17] For a young woman twenty years old, it must have been singularly unromantic and quite strange, but "everything was strange then."[18]

The next morning, they informed the Sandilands and David wrote to tell his parents. After Rosemary told her admirer, Tony Lock, that she was engaged and sent him back to Scotland, she consulted her tutor, Hugh Gaitskell, who was serving in the Ministry for Economic War. Gaitskell came to lunch with David, Rosemary, and her parents. She always said later that she asked Gaitskell whether she should complete her university education (she had only another year left) or, instead, leave to get married; Gaitskell encouraged her to marry.

It seems more likely that she had made up her own mind because she was already engaged to David when she talked to Gaitskell. The students at "University College were being sent out of London [because of the War]. I didn't want to go off." Her friends were going into the Red Cross or joining the Wrens (Women's Royal Naval Service), the ATS (Women's Auxiliary Territorial Service), or the WAAF (Women's Auxiliary Air Force). It was "a change in the way of life. I wanted to be part of life. He [Gaitskell] came to lunch. He thought it better to get married. I am deeply grateful to him forever."[19]

Today it is difficult to understand why Rosemary felt there had to be a choice between marriage and completing her degree. However, even in the absence of war, a young lady was not expected to pursue a college or university degree, or ever have a job. The First World War and the ensuing Depression meant there had not been enough jobs to go around for the men. In 1936, there was a march down Whitehall by ex-servicemen to protest the employment of married women. In most cases, if a woman married, she either quit or was fired. "That's why Teacher is always 'Miss.'"[20] Upper-class women never worked; it would have taken bread away from those who needed jobs to support a family. A woman's destiny during that era was to get married.

Thus Rosemary's formal education came to an end earlier than expected and without a degree. In David Farquharson's view, "I don't think this was any kind of a passionate affair. It happened with quite a lot of young couples. The War came on. They realized that if they were going to get married, now was the time because there would probably be no second chance. And there might be no men left. A lot of people married that first year in the War because they thought they would never get another chance."

Memories of the slaughter of the First World War were still fresh. A generation of young men had been killed leaving more than two million surplus women without husbands. Both men and women felt the need to marry and have children before it was too late. Under the circumstances, David offered a suitable match and although not particularly dashing or handsome, he was intellectual and good company as well as a close friend of Rosemary's favorite brother who was also about to marry. Rosemary acknowledged the pressure to have children, recalling, "He was an only son and was extremely fond of his father and mother, who were longing for him to get married and have a family. I fitted the bill . . . my job was to have children for David and his parents."[21]

David had to clear his marriage with his officers who advised him to proceed as soon as possible. He also had the "most intimate and perfect talk with Mum on a walk. . . . She has quite come round to the necessity of haste in our marriage. She was most understanding."[22] He does not mention his father. In very short order the plans proceeded, guests were invited, and wedding gifts received.

Rosemary and David were married on October 21, 1939, at St. James's, Piccadilly. The *Sunday Times* reported the next day that "Lieutenant David C. W. Verey, only son of Reverend Cecil H. and Mrs. Verey of Barnsley Close had married Miss Rosemary Sandilands, younger daughter of Lieutenant Colonel and Mrs. Prescott Sandilands of Coleherne Court." David's father officiated, accompanied by Archdeacon Lambert and Reverend Brian Green. "The bride . . . wore a gown of gold brocade, a Honiton lace veil and wreath of orange blossom and carried a sheath of lilies. She had three bridesmaids." David observed that "the church was beautifully decorated and everyone enjoyed the music and the service more than somewhat. The church was full. Dad married us and Brian Green gave the address. Reception lunch afterwards. I felt quite calm and enjoyed every minute."[23]

In what seems an odd choice of venue, the newlyweds spent their honeymoon at Barnsley where David's parents lived, although his parents had the good sense to move out for that time. There followed a round of parties as Rosemary and David moved into a flat in Hounslow, a western borough of London, located by Rosemary's mother who also supplied them with a maid. Linda Verey wrote Rosemary a lovely letter saying how nice it was to have another child, which she signed, "Your devoted Mother." There were later visits to Barnsley, and David admitted it was the first time he had been on a horse for over a year and a half. Two months later, they celebrated Rosemary's twenty-first birthday.

Rosemary herself said, "I gave up college to become a full time wife. You had to make a decision because of the War.

It was a really dramatic moment. You thought the end of the world might come. Half of one's friends went off and you would pick up the newspaper and see they were dead. It was ghastly. . . . All these other people were rushing off thinking about what fun it would be to get married and I decided to marry David. I wasn't in love with him with this huge passion, like you would say you couldn't live without him. But I think that was a good thing. We always loved each other as friends and had a happy life."[24]

Family Life and a Shattering Accident
1939—1953

I belong to a generation, taught by my mother,
that you married someone and that was your life.
You took care of him. He came first.

HE NEWLYWEDS' LIFE in London soon came to an end when David was sent off to join his regiment. Rosemary went to live with his parents at Barnsley "when I was not following him around with his regiment, the Royal Fusiliers." Since having children was an important reason for their marriage, children began to arrive very soon, first Charles in 1940, followed by Christopher in 1942. David was eventually recognized for the highly intelligent man he was and "left his regiment and joined the top-secret Special Operations Executive [known as S.O.E.], which meant that I could no longer follow him around. I rented a cottage in Fairford."[1] David was sent off on assignments to Italy and North Africa.

For three long years after these early days, Rosemary was left on her own as head of her young family. She was apart from David again until he returned at the end of the war on Guy Fawkes Day, 1945. With her young sons, Rosemary left Barnsley House and hired "a real old-fashioned nanny to help manage the children."[2] According to custom she was referred to by her employer's last name as Nanny Verey, joining the young family and staying for the following sixteen years. Rosemary moved them all into a cottage she rented in Fairford, not far away from Barnsley and the larger town of Cirencester, in the lovely Cotswolds countryside about two hours drive west of London. It was "a tiny house, always an agony of cold."[3]

With most of the men gone, many of Rosemary's school friends joined the Wrens and other war-related organizations. Some even took on the jobs that became available with so many men off fighting. Had she chosen not to marry, or possibly married but gone on to complete her University degree, Rosemary's life might well have taken a very different tack. Instead, she embarked upon family life in the country. One of her American friends, Arthur Reynolds, observed that Rosemary really "withdrew and became a mom during the War."

With fuel in short supply, Rosemary enterprisingly began to drive a goat cart around the village of Fairford. Everyone had to do their part for the war. There was a major push to encourage people to grow vegetables. Almost everyone turned their flower gardens and lawns over to food production. Rosemary grew food for her own small family and probably shared some of her produce with her neighbors. A Mr. Wall from the next village came every Saturday to help her. She described him as "a countryman and a natural teacher ... he had me growing cabbages and leeks and taking cuttings of the chrysanthemum plants he had given me."[4]

At the end of the war in 1945, Winston Churchill was defeated by Clement Attlee and the Labour Party. To conservative Rosemary, "it seemed as if the bottom had dropped out of my world and that before long we might be a communist state. But there was always hope – and my seeds came up in spite of Attlee's theories."

When David returned from the war to resume his place in their lives, Rosemary found the adjustment difficult. Her own conventional upbringing required her to give up being in charge and defer to her husband, even though during his absence, she "had carved the roast. I had changed. . . . He had changed. And you had to say, right, I have married this man because I loved him and I must still love him and it worked all right. It was quite horrendous to be honest and truthful. You had to abdicate certain things."[5]

For someone of Rosemary's strength and independence, David's reappearance and reassertion as head of household must have been extremely painful. They barely knew each other when he went off to the S.O.E. shortly after their wedding. Before that, their courtship had been nonexistent, their marriage sudden, and their life together brief and interrupted by his duties with his regiment. Rosemary had grown from a young bride barely of twenty-one years to a mother of two in charge of everything.

"We were separated for three years. When he came back he was a stranger. I had been caring for his children, but I had organized my own life. I had become self-sufficient. While he was away, for example, I always carved the Sunday joint. During the War you only had two ounces of meat each and you had to be rather clever at carving. But men traditionally always do the carving. When he came home, I still wanted to go on doing it. But I belong to a generation, taught by my mother, that you married someone and that was your life. You took care of him. He came first."[6]

It must have been challenging for both of them. David had to adjust to civilian life and fit into his family. Rosemary recognized that it was "even more difficult for the men coming back. They had to get a job." Rosemary had to learn to defer to him, step back from being head of the household, let him take charge, and set the course for the family. His first thought was to resettle the family in London where he hoped to find a job as an architect. Had David managed to settle the family in London, as he tried to do, Rosemary might never have considered a garden. It would be David who took the family off to Gloucestershire, and David who would initiate the creation of their garden.

London had been devastated by the blitz. More than twenty thousand Londoners had been killed and large areas of the City completely destroyed by the bombings. The couple spent a few months there as David sought to find work. They "were shocked by the war damage in London. No new building was taking place; it was all repairing bombed buildings, using utility materials." But despite the need to rebuild huge areas of London, England was in the early stages of recovery, with food, fuel, and basic materials all severely rationed for the foreseeable future. The rebuilding concentrated on repairs and salvage, hardly challenging work for an aspiring young architect. Nor were there many jobs. Rosemary recalled that "although he was a qualified architect, the best salary he was offered was less than I paid my gardener, so he decided to accept a job from the Ministry of Housing as an investigator of historic buildings, listing these according to their architectural merit."[7]

Rosemary's future was completely dependent upon David's decision. When he was assigned to Gloucestershire and the adjoining counties, the family moved back to a home in the environs of Barnsley and Fairford. They left London never to return to live there again. David would remain in this post for almost twenty years, eventually writing two highly respected volumes of the Pevsner's Buildings of England series that are still in print.[8]

By contrast to the ravaged London, returning to the country must have seemed a deliverance. In the rural villages, life continued much as before. The Cotswold countryside, with its honey-gold stone buildings, gently rolling green hills with fields outlined by undulating stone walls, windbreak clumps of ancient trees, and hedgerows full of wildlife, was dotted with picturesque small villages, supporting an agricultural way of life. For most of the populace, life centered on their crops and their livestock. A strong class system persisted, with the upper crust still living in the manor houses and riding their horses and dogs in the hunt. The Church was at the core of village life, its steeple rising above the surrounding buildings. David was to study and inventory many of these historic churches in his new work.

David and Rosemary bought a handsome stone house called Hinton House in the village of Ablington, only a few miles down the road from the village of Barnsley. The house suited their needs. It had a lawn for the children that sloped down from the front door toward a lavender hedge, as well as a tennis court and a small paddock. As a passionate horsewoman and competitive tennis player, Rosemary felt that the house clearly met her requirements for happiness. Three loose box stalls held her horse and ponies for the children. They moved in December 20, 1946, the day before her twenty-eighth birthday. One wing served as the nursery where Nanny Verey could attend to the children, while Rosemary and David had their privacy and were left undisturbed. While Rosemary did continue to gain some experience growing vegetables at Hinton House, she focused her energies on her children, her horses, tennis, and other conventional social pursuits expected of a good church-going mother and wife.

Soon thereafter, their daughter Veronica was born in 1946, followed by Davina in 1949. Rosemary's life took on the typical rhythm of an English country lady who, although not aristocracy, fit into upper-class country life or what one American friend dubbed the "squierarchy." Nanny Verey helped rear the four young children while the Master and Mistress entertained in traditional style. As was true (and is still often true) of English country houses, Hinton House was barely heated and Gillian Sandilands remembered it "was an agony of uncomfortableness." Nevertheless, following strict social conventions, the dinner guests at Hinton House were expected to appear in black tie. On one particularly stormy and cold weekend, the arriving guests had to walk over duckboards to avoid the floodwaters and get to the front door. Gillian, arriving from London, was quite unprepared for formal dress. "If it was a freezing cold house and flooded, you would not have thought it was the moment for black tie. I always used to wear [my husband's] socks in bed."

Both Rosemary and David hunted, although Rosemary with much more enthusiasm, greater skill, and more daring. The Church was at the center of their lives; David and Rosemary assumed important responsibilities that seemed only fitting for the son of a Vicar. David's work took him traveling all around Gloucestershire and the nearby counties. In addition to parties and dinners, their social life included tennis and fox hunting. If nothing out of the ordinary had occurred, Rosemary would have lived a comfortable, conventional country life, unnoticed by the larger world.

In 1951, just five years after their move to Hinton House, David's parents, Cecil and Linda Verey, decided to move into The Close, adjacent to Barnsley House, and give the main house to David. Rosemary and David sold Hinton House and moved into Barnsley, where they would live for the rest of their lives. The Close, originally a small stable and garage, was renovated for David's parents. The young Verey family of six, plus Nanny Verey, moved into the main house. Rosemary's godmother, Isabel Tait, sent them a large van full of antique furniture. "Thank Goodness," said Rosemary, "I taught David the difference between good and second-rate furniture!" She felt David was reluctant to criticize his parents' taste but that "his father went for the best, his mother the least expensive."[9] Given her own high standards, Rosemary was not one to settle for second best.

Barnsley House was a large, handsome, stone manor house dating from the William and Mary period that had served as a rectory but was privately owned when Cecil Verey acquired it in 1939 for his retirement. On subsequent garden tours, Rosemary never failed to point out the 1697 date carved in stone over the garden door with the initials B. B. for Brereton Bourchier, Squire of Barnsley, who built the house out of locally quarried, golden Cotswold stone. Eventually the Bourchier family moved on to build a far grander house in Barnsley Park on the northern outskirts of the village. Extensions to the 1697 building were added in the 1880s. Rosemary observed that the history of the house made her feel "ageless. This house has been here three hundred years. I'm a passing phase."[10]

For someone of his class and educational background, it was perhaps predictable that David would have very little interest in financial matters: his interests were far more intellectual. David's work for the Ministry of Housing did not pay handsomely, but as the only child in the extended Verey family, David inherited not only from his parents, but from his many childless uncles and aunts as well. Periodically, the financial coffers of the Vereys would be topped up by these inheritances. "He was always getting the jackpot every time." Gillian Sandilands observed that David "wasn't at all a striving person. You see, he always had just enough money not to have to bother. I mean if he had more money he would have done something more with it . . . and if he had less he would have had to do something about it, wouldn't he?"

It is hard to know what goes on inside any marriage, especially between two people with as different temperaments as David and Rosemary. Her friend the sculptor, Simon Verity, believed that Rosemary "genuinely adored David. He wasn't really man enough for her in some ways. She was just fierce and he was just gentle and intellectual and a little vague." Another friend, Arthur Reynolds, thought it "immediately obvious that Rosemary was the masculine force and David was the feminine force in the couple. He had a high-pitched voice that was very recessive. His passion was for architecture, but he had no idea about money and he thought it was vulgar to discuss it." David and Rosemary were "friends. It was a deep friendship but Rosemary made no secret of her affairs with lots of men that took her fancy. She didn't see in David a great love in that sense. She saw them as two people who were getting on in life together and making it work together. . . . I think it was conventional in a certain element, a certain intellectual element."

It was not unusual for established couples in certain circles to indulge in extramarital affairs, sometimes with the acknowledgement and acceptance of the other spouse. Often these affairs were homosexual in nature. Vita Sackville-West and Harold Nicolson were a well-known example, as well as the Vereys' close friends and neighbors, James and Alvilde Lees-Milne.[11] If Rosemary did have lovers, there was never any rupture in her marriage.

Rosemary herself acknowledged that theirs was a deep friendship rather than a passionate love match. But if the gossip about her affairs is at all true, nothing has publicly surfaced or come to light.[12] Perhaps Rosemary herself enjoyed encouraging others to conjure up these alliances. To some extent, it may have been her passion for horses and her love of the hunt that led to such speculation. The English maintain that "hunting and adultery go together like eggs and bacon."

Shortly after moving into Barnsley House, Rosemary grassed over her mother-in-law's flower borders, although her in-laws were living right next door in the attached Close. She did leave a small corner for them to enjoy. But where there had once been formal borders of roses, ponies and children now frolicked instead. Rosemary had no second thoughts, feeling the substitution of grass for flower borders allowed "more space for the children to play croquet, cricket and all their other things on the lawn."[13] She also concluded that with a lack of gardeners, her mother-in-law's herbaceous borders had grown "a bit weedy" and that they "were too large and too far from the house to be thoroughly enjoyed."[14]

Instead, Rosemary and David concentrated their attentions on building a tennis court and adding a swimming pool. On a typical day, they invited local friends to come for a day of tea, tennis, and dinner. Christopher Verey recalls that he and his siblings could never beat his mother at tennis. Not until she played with her grandchildren did she finally concede defeat: rather than risk losing, the ever-competitive Rosemary gave up the sport completely.

Rosemary was not alone in grassing over an existing garden. "After the War, people went back to the great houses, the manor houses. But they were faced with no servants in the house, and how would they live? Most of them just contracted back and couldn't cope. And then the gardens. They turfed them over. It was contraction, contraction."[15] People were learning to make do, to live without the support of servants, or at least without as many as before. Penelope Hobhouse, who became a famous garden writer and designer herself, recalled, "After the War people gave up. People like my parents-in-law just gave up." One of the first things they abandoned was the labor-intensive garden.

According to custom, and as is still the case for people in a certain slice of British society, Rosemary and David sent their sons away to school at the ages of eight and ten shortly before moving into Barnsley House. The boys lived at Heatherdown, their "public school" in Ascot, and came home only on holidays; they were not permitted to go home for the weekend. Eventually Charles and Christopher would go on at the appropriate ages to attend Eton, as their father had before them.

Girls were a different matter. Rosemary decided to keep her daughters at home and teach them herself. Her daughter Veronica recalls that many girls of families in the grand houses of the countryside were kept at home with a governess to teach them suitable social skills along with their lessons. The Vereys were in no position to hire a governess, so Rosemary took on the role herself, using a syllabus provided by the Parents' National Education Union to help Britons living abroad in the extended Commonwealth deliver a proper English education to children in countries without a suitable English school.

Gillian Sandilands recalled that Rosemary had enough confidence to think that "she could teach anything." From her military childhood and her own years at Eversley School, Rosemary remembered and insisted on "very strict discipline – 9 A.M. until 5 P.M., but with regular breaks and time for ponies. The first ten minutes were for exercises to warm us up, then Bible reading and on to history, geography, and current affairs." Rosemary learned along with her daughters. "I learnt more during the 1950s than I ever did ... in the years to come."[16]

In looking back, Rosemary described herself as an "obe-dient wife. I don't know if I was a good mother."[17] When she later asked her daughters their views on home schooling, she found that it had pros and cons. The children didn't learn to rub shoulders or socialize with other children. Pos-sibly it made them more inhibited and maybe shy. On the other hand, she believed they discovered it is fun to learn, and in order to learn, they had to concentrate on what they were doing. Focus and concentration would always be important to anything Rosemary undertook.

Her younger daughter, Davina, described her childhood as "very old fashioned . . . a mix of almost post-war progres-sion with a hint of pre-war (almost pre-First World War) life style. I didn't go to school until I was nine [and Veronica almost twelve] . . . most of our time was spent out of doors. My parents' relationship with employees and children was both intimate and distant at the same time. There was still a lack of equality that is hard to imagine nowadays; although society had started to change, Gloucestershire was still a backwater." Davina thought Rosemary had a very natural way with her children and was "a very common-sense mother," but she could also be demeaning. Given her own high stan-dards, Rosemary must have been a demanding and tough tutor for her girls. Years later, when she was quite frail, she was still chastising Davina in front of company for failing to load the dirty plates in the dishwasher exactly as required.

Rosemary and David had different priorities. For David, the hunt was a way of life rather than a pleasure, but for Rosemary it was her passion. While David rode well, he never enjoyed the hard work of grooming the horses and pulling on his boots. Rosemary loved to ride and found the hunt exhilarating. She believed "that hunting develops a spirit of independence. You are out in the countryside, suddenly alone. Who will help you? You must follow your own line if you wish to survive."[18]

But it proved to be a horse that almost killed her. In 1953, Rosemary had a serious accident that would change her life. She and a friend were getting some horses ready for the Christmas hunting when Rosemary mounted a horse not yet fully broken. "It reared over backwards so swiftly that I was still in the saddle as it fell," Rosemary recounted. When Rosemary was extracted from underneath the horse that had rolled over on her, they discovered that among her injuries, she had a badly smashed femur. She was sent off to the hospital with an injury so severe it required a plate to be inserted. She was in traction for over three months. It was not clear if she would ever walk again.

With the boys safely away at school, David took the girls and Nanny Verey to live with Rosemary's parents in London while Rosemary remained in the hospital in traction. She recalled, "Pain is difficult to remember once it leaves you, but I do remember the pain."[19] When she returned home, she refused to give up riding entirely. Never prone to complaining or sharing her inner feelings, Rosemary was always matter of fact in recounting this episode even though her injuries would adversely affect her health later in life. She continued to ride and hunt, although perhaps with a bit less enthusiasm and greater caution. As someone who never enjoyed doing anything by halves, she eventually gave it up entirely, leaving a void in her life that allowed her interest in the garden to grow.

ABOVE: *His Royal Highness The Prince of Wales greeting Rosemary Verey as she alights from a small plane for her eightieth birthday celebration. December 1998.*

BELOW: *Rosemary Verey in the Laburnum Walk at Barnsley House.*

LEFT: *The Sandilands family:*
Prescott and Gladys Sandilands with
their four children, Pat, Francis,
Christina, and Rosemary (in riding
clothes).

BELOW: *The wedding of David Verey*
and Rosemary Sandilands at St.
James, London, October 21, 1939.

RIGHT: *Portrait by*
N. Lytton of Rosemary
with her two sons,
Charles and Christopher,
1944.

ABOVE: *The Verey family: David and Rosemary Verey with their four children, Charles, Christopher, Veronica, and Davina.*

BELOW: *David and Rosemary at Barnsley House in the 1950s, before there were any gardens.*

ABOVE: *Rosemary, a passion-ate hunter, jumping on Mata Hari.*

LEFT: *David and Rosemary at Barnsley House in front of the covered verandah where the Knot Garden would be.*

CHAPTER THREE

Creating the Garden
1960s

*In a garden you get what
you work for, don't you?*

T WAS DAVID who pushed Rosemary into creating a garden at Barnsley. He first piqued her interest in the subject by buying and presenting her with old gardening books he acquired on his travels for the Ministry of Housing. He loved books himself, particularly the books he collected for his own scholarly work on the architectural history of Gloucestershire. He introduced Rosemary to the classical Greek and Roman writers, the likes of Theophrastus, Dioscorides, and Pliny, whose writings about plants influenced medieval science and medicine, along with the early herbalists who became her favorites, such as William Turner, John Gerard, and John Parkinson.

"With his understanding of Rosemary and her mathematical, geometric mind, [David] was able to nudge her. He was really a great bibliophile. He had a lot of books on Gloucestershire. He started to buy her ancient books on gardening. I think he could see that with these fifteenth- and sixteenth-century treatises . . . she could have a lot of fun and really make a niche for herself, which indeed she did."[1] After dinner, Rosemary would curl up in her chair for hours before the fire, sitting companionably with David while immersed in some large tome about gardens. These old herbals were hard to read but offered a window into the past, appealing to Rosemary's interest in history and her fascination with classical patterns and designs.

The older Vereys had died not many years after giving Barnsley to David, first David's mother in 1956 and then his father in 1958.[2] David decided it was time to replace the garden that Rosemary had grassed over soon after they moved into Barnsley House. Perhaps he wished to pay tribute to his mother's memory or perhaps, because the girls had gone away to board at St. Mary's Calne School, he realized there was no longer any need for grassy playing fields. Whatever the reason, David chose not to wait for Rosemary to move ahead with this idea.[3]

But he did ask her what she proposed to do in order to occupy the time formerly spent on teaching the girls. Rosemary, still sufficiently engaged with riding and having groomed her own horses and kept the tack clean for years, asked for a full-time groom. David complied and turned his parents' residence in The Close into groom's quarters. Later, however, Rosemary would say that she began to tire of riding. "It became a way of life rather than an occasional pursuit. I realized then that I did not want to devote the rest of my life from September until March to hunting."[4]

The timing was perfect. Rosemary was at loose ends without her daughters at home to teach, and her energies needed some outlet. She recognized that "one of the worst things about getting married and having children is that all you know about is washing nappies and ironing clothes. Unless you are exceptional, you realize you are becoming dull."[5] With a nanny and other help in the house, it is unlikely that Rosemary spent much of her time washing nappies or ironing clothes, but she firmly believed, and often said, "It's a sin to be dull!"

With Rosemary still engaged with horses and hunting, David moved to re-establish a decent garden around their house. Without consulting Rosemary, or possibly because she expressed no interest in his undertaking, David pressed ahead. He started by focusing on the area immediately around the house and called Percy Cane, a fashionable garden designer of the day, to come to Barnsley.

Percy Cane was known for an Arts and Crafts approach to garden design, which was of keen interest to David. The Cotswolds had been at the heart of the movement that began in the late 1800s and continued into the early part of the twentieth century. Reacting to the industrialization taking place in England, and influenced by writers like John Ruskin, the movement counted William Morris among its leading proponents, advocating a return to traditional architecture and crafts produced by hand rather than by machines. His home, Kelmscott Manor, was in Lechlade, not far from Barnsley, and several prominent like-minded architects followed him to the area.[6]

Given his own interest in the Arts and Crafts movement, it was natural for David to engage a garden designer who championed it. When Percy Cane arrived at Barnsley without any warning, "Rosemary saw red! She'd been resisting. You can see her – eyes lighting up with fury. Getting in someone else in when she was going to do it and she did."[7]

Rosemary admitted Cane's arrival "was most provocative to me. I realized that it was my garden,"[8] so Percy Cane was quickly ushered back to London. No one was going to tell her what to do about her own garden. With her back up, she was determined to take charge. Looking back, Rosemary gave Percy Cane credit for teaching her one important lesson, namely "that you should always make the longest possible distance into your most important vista and give it an interesting focal point." And it taught her another useful lesson. Remembering her own reaction, Rosemary believed that any garden she later designed had to be the client's garden, not hers.

Before Percy Cane was sent packing, he did suggest the basic outline for the borders just outside the south-facing door of the drawing room at Barnsley House. Here, years before, Linda Verey had planted parallel rows of tall Irish yews, marching like stiff green sentinels along the path that led away from that door out to a gate that opened through an existing stone wall to the farm lane beyond. In the 1770s, an early owner, the Reverend Charles Coxwell, had built a high stone wall on three sides of the grounds, starting at the southeastern end, turning to run along the south and then turning back again. A small Gothic Revival-style garden-house remained at this northern end of the wall, serving as a full stop feature and garden folly. Beyond the end of the garden wall, a yew hedge hid the swimming pool Rosemary and David had built at the furthest northwestern edge.

Although Rosemary had not eliminated the tall yews when she grassed over the gardens of her mother-in-law, there was only grass on either side of the yews when Percy Cane arrived. In place of open lawn, Percy Cane outlined four symmetrical triangular beds on either side of the yew-lined central path. Each triangle had a gentle curving hypotenuse to contrast to the sharp right angles of the other two sides. This design, quite simple but classical, was appropriate to the age and architecture of the house. The four beds, later called the Parterres, would become the heart of Rosemary's garden at the rear of Barnsley House.

Originally, the farm lane just beyond the stone wall had served as the main village thoroughfare, but after the intro-duction of the automobile, a broader paved parallel road had been built further north. As a result, the drawing room door looking out over the Parterres and the yew walk toward the farm lane beyond would once have been the front entrance of the house. Instead, after the paved road arrived, the north facing façade became the front entrance, facing this main road that connected the important town of Cirencester to the south with the charming village of Bibury to the north and continued on through the heart of the Cotswolds. A handsome pair of iron gates connected the driveway to this busily trafficked road. Alongside the driveway's edge, another stone wall ran uphill to the house, behind a row of handsome large trees; in early spring, the ground is awash with aconites blooming a sea of yellow. Linda Verey had planted formal herbaceous borders in the front of the house, where the sloping land had been terraced. In her eradication phase, Rosemary eliminated these borders and simplified the terraces, leaving an unfussy, quiet green area at the front entrance of the handsome three-story house.

Before Cane's arrival, Rosemary already had begun experimenting with a few plantings of trees and shrubs at the southwestern edge of lawn, just beyond the Gothic Revival gardenhouse, with no formal wall or enclosure there other than the yew hedge hiding the pool. She described this area "as somewhere between a woodland and a wild flower meadow."[9] She called it the Wilderness. The very name suggests the influence of William Robinson, whose influential book, *The Wild Garden*, and later writings passionately called for a more natural approach to gardening in England. Robinson, who was influenced by John Ruskin as well as the American Frederick Law Olmsted, would have been embraced by anyone like David Verey interested in the Arts and Crafts movement.

Rejecting the Victorian gardening style of bedding-out

tender plants in highly formal, geometric-shaped areas, William Robinson preached a more naturalistic and picturesque approach. Rosemary wrote about this shift in gardening style away from the formal bedding-out of tender plants, noting "William Robinson crusaded to change the fashion to a more permanent mixed and herbaceous border."[10] Robinson was an important influence on Major Lawrence Johnston, an American who created his magnificent gardens at Hidcote Manor in Gloucestershire, not far from Barnsley. Hidcote was certainly known to Rosemary. Further away in Kent, Vita Sackville-West's gardens at Sissinghurst Castle and her widely read garden writings were also influenced by Robinson's views.

Given her own early university studies in social history, Rosemary was well aware that styles evolve, and from her library, that garden styles were no exception. "Like cooking, gardening is tremendously influenced by social history. At the turn of the century, cheap labor and cheap coal meant people could have fleets of gardeners and enormous hothouses. Because lots of exotics were coming into this country from around the world, extra flowerbeds were created to fit everything in. In those times, the ladies of the house often knew little of their garden. Now that situation has changed and in many cases for the better."[11]

Like any beginning amateur, Rosemary's first efforts in her wilderness were not too successful. As a novice, she began to regularly attend the Royal Horticultural Society flower shows at Vincent Square in London and visited many gardens, taking constant notes. Absorbed by trees and shrubs, she wisely consulted a tree expert, Tim Sherrard, at a local nursery. In contrast to her later, more effective, formal areas of her garden, The Wilderness was rarely noticed or photographed, probably because it wasn't much more than a collection of fine but somewhat randomly placed trees without any structure, vista or focal point.

In due course, Rosemary herself admitted that the Wilderness was not something she took great pride in, much as she continued to admire many of the plants there. "Now inevitably, I would like to treat a few (trees) as chessmen and move them round the board. . . . I would do at least three of each crab and cherry instead of a single to make a bolder accent. These mistakes are the price paid for an amateur instead of a professional layout."[12] However, this particular amateur was a keen observer and critic of her own efforts, learning from these early experiences.

By Christmas of 1961, Rosemary was far enough along in gardening that her daughter Davina gave her a book to serve as a garden journal. Rosemary knew enough about the growing conditions in her garden to remember "My daughter gave me a notebook importantly titled 'Gardening Book' on the opening page; below I added the words: 'Be not tempted by plants that hate lime.'"[13] The following year, her son Charles gave her a membership in the Royal Horticultural Society. Although she continued to enjoy her horses and tennis, she faced a steep learning curve in the garden. As she learned about plants, she was fortunate to have David bring his architectural talents to bear on providing the bones of the place.

In 1962 David placed a jewel in the garden. He acquired a small, classically styled Temple, suffering from years of disrepair and neglect at nearby Fairford Park. He had it moved stone by stone to Barnsley where he sited it just behind an existing reflecting pool located in a walled corner off to the east side of the Parterres. This corner of the garden had served as his parents' private retreat during the years they lived in The Close. After their death, David had installed this small pond to replace what had been his parents' lawn. By chance, the measurements of the elegant Temple perfectly aligned with the width of the pool and anchored one end of the garden with a beautifully proportioned set piece of formal architecture. In hindsight Rosemary observed, "Men gardeners will do things like moving temples. I wouldn't have done that and I don't think [David] would have been all that good at designing borders."[14]

David also rescued a set of iron railing with double gates which he placed in front of the Temple with its pool to create a sense of enclosure; he chose to paint it a surprising but pleasant deep blue, the perfect foil for the profusion of plants that Rosemary would add to scramble through it.

David then planted an avenue of lime trees (*Tilia platyphyllos* 'Rubra') in line with the Temple leading away toward the garden wall at the far western end. Because there are no straight lines in old houses, David soon realized that his parallel rows of nine lime trees seemed to veer off sideways because the old stone wall running alongside was not truly parallel to the house causing his trees to run off at a slight angle. Correction came in the form of optical illusion or an architectural trick. Nicholas Ridley, their local Member of Parliament and a grandson of the late, revered architect, Sir Edwin Lutyens, gave "an instant pronouncement. Plant another line of limes!"[15] And plant them to compensate for the problem by slowly increasing the space between each tree in the double row. To the untutored eye, these two rows of limes, one a single row and the other a double, now appear to be perfectly straight.

To complete this avenue effect, Rosemary asked her brother Francis and his wife Gill for a gift of laburnums and wisterias. Or to be more precise, Rosemary ordered the plants and informed the Sandilands that these plants would be their anniversary gift. "I have bought as a silver wedding present from you, Francis, ten Laburnum and ten Wisterias for an extension to David's lime avenue. When the bill comes I will send it to you! I think it might be quite something one day!"[16] It was just like Rosemary not only to expect a gift but to dictate the choice and then buy it herself. She knew exactly what she wanted and made sure she got it. Indeed her words proved to be prophetic. The laburnum allée would not only "be quite something one day," it would become one of the most photographed and iconic of garden images.

Where did this idea of a laburnum allée come from? Certainly the magnificent one at Bodnant, now a National Trust property in Wales, was well known at the time. Given its grand scale and fame, it is hard to think that its existence wasn't at least known to Rosemary. But she claimed not to have been influenced by the Bodnant laburnums, nor to have seen them before she created her own, or "ours might have been wider."[17] She credits instead Russell Page's *Education of a Gardener*, published in 1962, for causing her to think about focal points and a long axis, something that was sorely missing in her Wilderness.

Nearer to home, Nancy Lancaster – living at Haseley Court in neighboring Oxfordshire – had also created a beautiful laburnum walk in her own garden. Nancy Lancaster was an American living in England with a great sense of style. She became well known for founding the decorating firm of Colefax and Fowler, which promoted the "English country house" style in furnishings and fabrics. One of Rosemary's gardeners, Nick Burton, would later observe, "The lovely irony is it took an American [Nancy Lancaster] to teach the English how to decorate their houses." Rosemary certainly knew and must have been influenced by Nancy who would later be among the women featured in Rosemary's first book.

Did either or both of these earlier laburnum walks inspire Rosemary's choice? While it is impossible to know, Rosemary does not credit either source, although she was usually generous in acknowledging the influence of others. Her own garden designs are not necessarily original. What Rosemary did do, and do brilliantly, was to adapt existing designs and make them fit into her relatively small garden, there to be enriched by her extraordinary sense of color and stunning profusion of plants. First-time visitors to Barnsley are often surprised when they see how small the scale actually is of this oft-photographed laburnum walk. There are only five laburnums on either side of the path and wisteria was planted to climb through each laburnum, adding their touch of purple flowers to mix and bloom simultaneously with the yellow laburnums. She underplanted the row with the purple globes of *Allium aflatunense* to complete the picture. This vision of yellow and mauve blooming together for almost three weeks every year called for a high degree of horticultural skill to insure all the plants were happy, and that the wisteria didn't strangle the laburnum.

The composition was perfected when David added his quite original rough pebble path beneath the pendulous blossoms of laburnum and wisteria. David's travels for the Housing Ministry took him as far afield as Wales, and he loved to swim, often visiting the Welsh beaches where he picked up stones and carried them home in the trunk of his car. He then spent hours painstakingly setting each small stone in cement by hand to create an uneven walk. To at least one observer, this entire enterprise seemed bizarre and the path appeared impossible to walk on. But David's pebble path added an idiosyncratic, delightful touch to the laburnum allée. "It all looked so homespun as to be ridiculous. Anyone would trip over these huge pebbles with lots of space in between, but in fact it works. It's great. It's unusual."[18]

Shortly before David retired from his position as senior investigator of historic buildings in 1965, he bought and restored a derelict mill that was little more than a shell in the next village of Arlington into a small, private museum. Because of his interest in architectural history and in particular, the history of the Cotswolds and the Arts and Crafts movement, he wanted to display artifacts alongside local crafts. The museum was quirky and original, containing all the things he loved. He had spent many years studying, cataloging, and grading the handsome stone churches of Gloucestershire, the so-called Wool Churches built in the fifteenth and sixteenth centuries by fortunes made from sheep and the wool trade. After retiring, he had the time to spend on his museum as well as his own writing. He wrote a Shell Guide to Gloucestershire in addition to the two volumes he had produced for the Pevsner's buildings series.[19]

For opening day of the museum, David invited a young sculptor, Simon Verity, to carve an inscription outside the door to attract people to come. Simon's uncle, Oliver Hill, was a distinguished architect and knew David slightly from those circles. Simon quickly saw that he was "the carver and the act." Rosemary admired his talents, and Simon's wonderful statues, plinth, and fountain would later add important dimensions to the developing gardens at Barnsley.

In 1968, David was appointed High Sheriff of Gloucestershire. That office dates back to the tenth century and exists to this day as a royal appointment of great prestige and honor. The High Sheriff represents the Crown in overseeing law and order but more as a formality than a reality. Over the centuries as the professional police force developed, the office of High Sheriff had become largely ceremonial. In David's year, he had to attend countless openings, dedications, and similar activities occurring throughout the County. He also had to equip himself with the appropriate dress to suit his title and to greet and host various visiting dignitaries, all at his own expense.

Rosemary served as his official consort and hostess. Since David was always a fairly private person, in contrast to Rosemary who always loved a party, some close observers believed that she might well have preferred to hold the title herself. "Rosemary secretly felt that she was at least half of the equation although the role was his," her assistant, Katherine Lambert, observed.

Rosemary admitted that she intentionally deferred to David. The garden became her place to shine. "With my husband I always played my success very low key on purpose, because he was the clever one. That was how I saw it and that was the way I played it. He was full of charm and everybody loved him. But he wasn't a natural in the garden. That was my area."[20] She was not alone. As with so many women before her, the garden had an emancipating effect. It was "a domain in the pre-feminist era which they could set out to conquer, and they did," observed the historian Jenny Uglow.[21] Although at this early stage, Rosemary never thought of making it her career, she knew herself well enough to admit that when she did something, she did it wholeheartedly.

Looking back on their partnership, Rosemary was insightful about the different roles she and David played in creating their garden. After the war and the loss of the head gardener, she asked, "Who has taken charge of the garden? It's usually the woman of the house. And this has been a way for her to express her artistic talents. She's learned about plants and she's learned about color coordination and she's really enjoyed doing it." Then with a slightly annoyed tone of voice, she noted, "Usually, it's the man who has control of the money!" Hence it is the man who says, "Why don't we plant an avenue, why don't we make a lake, why don't we change the drive, and he is in the position to be able to do the much more hard landscaping, the things that are going to be more expensive to do."[22] Certainly this was the case here with David in control of the money and David focusing on the architectural features of their garden.

David also assumed important leadership roles in the Church, serving on the Diocesan Advisory Committee, a highly regarded position. Eventually he became Chair of that committee, a position he held for seventeen years. Rosemary joined him in her commitment to the church. They both served as warden at various times and Rosemary arranged and delivered flowers faithfully every week. Members of the congregation found it very hard to say no to Rosemary when she decided they should perform some service. Once when Anne de Courcy, the parishioner Rosemary had selected to write a history of the church, hesitated, "her eyes swiveled around . . . in that well known way . . . and after a direct gaze from Rosemary," she capitulated.

When the church meetings were in the evening, Rosemary could become confrontational, especially when she had been drinking. She could be prickly, but at least she was also self-aware. Anne recalls she acknowledged that, "If I'm on anything, I feel I have to run it. I feel I have to be Queen Bee."

While Rosemary was busy supporting David in his High Sheriff role and in the governance of the Church, she continued to enhance her knowledge and horticultural skills. She began to learn about mixed borders, herbaceous plants, and spring bulbs. She had a misting system installed in one of the existing small greenhouses and started propagating plants there. Like any new enthusiast, she entered specimens of her plants into the RHS Flower Shows and competitions, winning a ribbon as a first-timer for one of her unusual willows from the Wilderness (*Salix daphnoides aglaia*). She continued to read voraciously – especially more contemporary books – visited gardens, took notes, and listened to the advice of others.

One local plant mentor was Nancy Lindsay, the only child of Norah Lindsay, who had been a socially prominent, much-sought-after garden designer before her death in 1948. Along with her mother, Nancy had been a close friend of Major Lawrence Johnston, the creator of Hidcote, where she ran a small nursery. Hidcote is now one of the star properties owned by the National Trust. Lawrence left his other garden in France (called Serre de la Madone) to Nancy when he died. Rosemary visited Nancy at the garden her mother Norah had created at The Manor House at Sutton Courtenay where she made copious notes. One important precept Nancy taught Rosemary was to start by growing easy plants, so she would be gratified by the results. Then she could increase her repertoire, expanding into rarer and more exotic species. It was wise advice to use plants that would thrive and flourish, rather than starting out with finicky rarities that would likely die. Nancy sold Rosemary hardy geraniums, hellebores, hostas, and other similar good plants, suggesting that rare treasures could be tried by tucking them in among these strong performers.

Although Percy Cane had urged her to always create vistas using the longest axis across the garden, it took Rosemary quite a long time to comply. Finally in 1968, she opened a vista that began at the Temple and continued for over one hundred yards to the old stone wall at the opposite end. She removed an old lonicera hedge and other obstructing plantings, which were replaced with a wide grassy walk, flanked on one side by the limes and laburnums and the other by a newly developing area Rosemary called her long border. Acknowledging Gertrude Jekyll's advice, Rosemary incorporated yellows in this border, to "create a feeling of sunlight. A glowing yellow took over what had once been drab and was now alive."

By the end of the 1960s, Rosemary felt confident enough about her developing garden and skills to begin to write short articles for *The Countryman*. This was not a garden magazine per se, but a quarterly publication devoted to the issues surrounding rural life. *The Countryman* describes itself as "A Quarterly non-party review and miscellany of rural life and work for the English Speaking World." Published in Gloucestershire, *The Countryman*'s topics ranged from articles on birds, fishing, shooting, and decoys to advice for farmers, with a scattering of cartoons, often depicting oafish farmers.

Rosemary's first writings appeared in 1968 in a two-part article entitled "A Garden Inheritance" in which she described Barnsley's garden and its evolution. Crediting the influence of others and attending the Royal Horticultural Society shows at Vincent Square, she included practical advice along with her enthusiasm, noting how important it was to bear in mind the limey Cotswold soil. So began Rosemary's regular writing for *The Countryman*. She first wrote a couple of articles on her own garden before becoming a regular contributor, with several others, to a section entitled "Hints from the Home Acre." She usually wrote a short page or two on specific plant topics and how to grow them. She encouraged her readers to visit other gardens, as she had done herself when she began, and to keep notes of the plants coveted from a friend's garden, ones that have long summer bloom, prove reliable in the English "unsummery summers," require no staking, and prove to be good mixers.

Rosemary always took notes herself and encouraged her readers to do the same. "Good plant associations play a vital part in achieving a successful garden and creating them is a constant fascination. If you have kept an eye open for effective combinations in other people's gardens and remembered to make a note of them." She also used her eyes. "I have cut a stalk of ceanothus and carried it round the garden to find other good combinations."[23]

By 1970, Rosemary had her first article published in the prestigious magazine *Country Life*, writing about the fruits and flowers of Nassau after she and David had taken a trip there. Here, again, she followed David, for he had an article published in the magazine a year before and would have several more in 1970, 1971, and 1973 about historic churches, the Georgian buildings of Nassau, and related architectural topics. Her first article was a complement to David's; she'd have to wait nine years for a second appearance. But by that time, she wrote on her own.

In that same year of 1970, Rosemary turned fifty-two and opened her garden to the public for the first time. It was only for a single day as part of the National Gardens Scheme, but it was a start.

CHAPTER FOUR

Sharpening Her Art
1970s

It would be awful not to be wanted.

S IS TRUE of any personal garden, Rosemary's would evolve over time. At the start of the 1970s, the core of her garden was in place and maturing, but Rosemary would add some of its most distinctive features over the next decade, sharpening and refining her art. Drawing from her personal library of old herbals and garden books and her strong interest in garden history, she decided to add a knot garden, followed by an herb garden, and finally her influential potager. Each of these creations benefited from her love of geometrical patterns and was enriched by her deepening knowledge of plants.

When her house was built in 1697, formal gardens would have been in fashion and she felt, quite rightly, it was historically correct to design formal gardens to compliment the architecture of the house. Knot gardens, popular in Elizabethan times, had an interlacing of clipped herbs or shrubs within a square or rectangular framework. They were often planted in the shape of heraldic designs or made to mimic the patterns created by embroidery or oriental carpets. Ideally, the viewer would look down to "admire their knot gardens from a mount or a raised wall."[1] Rosemary was fascinated by the geometric possibilities of these designs and decided to create one at Barnsley.

In her library, she turned to Gervase Markham's *The Countrie Farm* (1616) as well as to *The Compleat Gardeners Practice* by Stephen Blake (1664) for ideas. She found examples in each book that could be copied on a small scale, and her mathematical skills allowed her to follow Gervase Markham's advice: "First make your design on paper and then superimpose grid lines. Using cord and pegs, stretch out this grid on the ground and copy the knot over it with a trail of dry sand." She sited her own knot garden just off the verandah on the western side of the house with its crenellated porch.

By the 1960s and 1970s, knot gardens had long been out of favor, people having lost interest and patience for these intricate affairs. In the early 1970s the Cotswolds were still pretty economically strapped. The oil crisis had rocked the stock markets and London was a dark city after the sun went down, as offices and homes switched off unnecessary lights to save energy. Although a time of public misery, Rosemary managed to go back to the source, synthesize the great forms, and scale them down to a workable size. She simply copied two of the most complex patterns from her books, reducing them to fit her space.

This was definitely a do-it-yourself affair. The two knot-pattern sections she planted are each only five yards square; they are surrounded by a yard of unplanted ground inside the outer hedge that provides the frame. When she realized how much hand clipping it took to keep a knot garden in crisp shape each year, she was retrospectively relieved that the space had dictated a relatively small design. "The whole beauty of the knots depends on how well tutored the box is kept, and I am thankful that we chose to place them where we did, in a space that restricted their size." Rosemary was pleased with the result, citing the great eighteenth-century English landscape designer, Humphry Repton, who had observed two centuries before that any plantings close to a house help keep it "anchored" into its surroundings. Rosemary's knots had become "almost a shadow of the house."[2]

Whenever she took visitors around the garden, she would often explain that historically the spaces between the threads of the knot were filled with colors to mark the particular heraldry of the design, although subsequently the spaces were sometimes infilled with flowering plants. Much as she loved her flower borders, she avoided planting any in her knot garden "so the pattern of the beds becomes the positive, and their formal shape the eyecatcher, and the infilling, visually, will be of secondary importance."[3]

She initially tried to follow Markham's recommendations to apply colors to the open earth between the threads of the knot's interweaving plants, using historically correct materials: finely ground Flanders tiles for red, sand for gold, coal dust for black, chalk for silver, and a mix of coal and chalk for blue. Always practical, she tried maintaining this standard, but the materials were difficult to obtain and keeping the pattern looking fresh required annual renewal. Eventually, she settled for local gravel. But her teaching instincts compelled her to explain the proper approach whenever she took visitors around the garden.

This design drawn from garden history had a handsome antique sundial standing at the entrance and was punctuated at each corner by four beautiful variegated hollies (*Ilex* × *altaclerensis* "Golden King") that Rosemary formed into topiaries, shaping each holly into two tiers of balls, one atop the other. The hollies were given to Rosemary by the head gardener at Bruern Abbey. As a young girl then helping Rosemary in the garden, Caroline Burgess, now head of Stonecrop, a public garden in Cold Spring, New York, remembers she was just learning to drive when Rosemary let her drive them over to Bruern Abbey. "It was . . . my first ride in the dark. And I was swerving because of the lights. I remember Rosemary . . . not quite shouting at me but quite stern as I swerved all over the road. You know of course that she could be stern."[4]

Caroline Burgess first came to Barnsley as a teenager passionate about horses to help with Davina's pony while Davina was away in school. She would bicycle over each day from her home in Cirencester several miles away. As Rosemary grew less interested in riding and more occupied with the garden, she asked her to pitch in and help. Originally paid twenty pence an hour, Caroline remembers that they worked from dawn to dusk without stop. She recalls it as Rosemary's "hay day," when she was out in the garden for hours on end, her hand in everything, making sure that it was perfect. New plants were continually being substituted for others removed, especially in the densely planted flower borders and the tubs near the house. Carolyn helped change the plants in those tubs two or three times a year. Being fully engaged in the garden all day, Rosemary got up very early in the morning to find time to read. She often told Caroline, "I had my best reading this morning at five o'clock."

Caroline recalls Rosemary insisting on the highest standards of maintenance, "walking up and down the borders, getting every bad leaf off of anything. I think it was immaculate! I think it was well presented, this incredible, immaculate garden showing what one individual can do with brains. I wouldn't say necessarily with money, she certainly wasn't extravagant. It was just hard, hard labor. She would push, push, push. I don't think there was any downtime. Totally flat out! And she went flat out. And she was happy to go flat out." Caroline saw her "on her hands and knees the whole time. In the dirt."

Although Rosemary was never seen in pants later in life,

Caroline remembers her dressed in "tartan plus-fours," a kind of pant ended tight at the knee. Americans would call these "knickers," although that would confuse the British who use that term for underwear. "She wore socks. Long stockings and these desert boots of suede. That's what she gardened in every single day until she graduated to a skirt. But she always had a pack of cigarettes in her hand, always. I remember her holding her cigarettes as she hoisted herself up on the various horses and put them through their paces. I was in awe." By sheer force of character, Rosemary decided one day to stop her chain-smoking habit. Caroline remembers she just said, "'This habit is disgusting.' And she said to David, 'We're stopping now.' And she just stopped. She was so proud that she could just stop. And David had to just stop too."

Encouraged by her successful knot garden, Rosemary went on to add an Herb Garden where she once again created patterns with low clipped box hedges that formed diamond-shaped spaces that she planted with herbs. Caroline recalls, "She had squared paper for the Knot Garden and for the Herb Garden. For the Herb Garden we even laid out sand to make those diamonds." Quite sensibly, she located her herb garden right outside her kitchen door, in order to provide easy access for a last-minute snip or two to add to the cooking pot. To do this, she had to carve out a slice from one of the existing Percy Cane Parterres, somewhat destroying the symmetry of the four main borders at the center of the garden. Walking through the densely planted garden, a visitor would be unlikely to notice what is essentially an odd add-on to the otherwise symmetrical four-bed design of the Parterres, but Rosemary, quite sensibly, wanted her herbs close at hand to the kitchen.

Writing about this, Rosemary said, "Secretly, I admire

people who make a real herb garden." Before she created her own, her herbs were scattered around "in every corner of the garden." She told herself that this allowed her to walk through and pick them at the last minute. But she had to admit, "I know that I am hoodwinking myself and the real reason is laziness."[5] There was nothing lazy about Rosemary, even though from time to time she mused about staying late in bed. "When my children were young and I had to get out of bed to make their breakfasts, I used to say: One day I will be able to lie in bed. Now I think: Luckily that day will never come. It would be awful not to be wanted."[6]

The patterns she created in her herb garden were again copied from designs she had seen, this time at nearby gardens in Fairford and at John and Marjorie Buxton's garden, Cole Park in Malmesbury. Even though the site she chose disrupted the integrity of the original plans, the herb garden provided an aesthetically pleasing way to grow herbs while keeping the unruliest of them disciplined within the confines of the tidy box hedge.

In 1972, David added another stunning piece of architecture to the garden in the form of a beautiful fountain that he commissioned as an anniversary gift. David asked Simon Verity to carve it to complete the end of the vista from the Temple down over the long grass walk and border to the garden wall. Simon made a relief carving of two Cotswold rams out of spangled Purbeck stone full of fossils to suggest a sheep's fleece that he set against the darker grey backdrop of Hornton stone, "which looks like lead when it is wet."[7] Rosemary was amazed that Simon, despite his slight, will-o'-the-wisp build, could maneuver such heavy blocks of stone.

Judith Verity, then Simon's wife, carved four fat frogs for the sides of the fountain to spout water up at the rams. This design celebrated the Gloucestershire history of wealth built on wool and the "Wool Churches" that David loved and showcased so avidly in his Arlington Museum. A decade after David brought the temple to Barnsley, Simon Verity's fountain provided the perfect full stop to the longest view in the garden. Rosemary often quoted Russell Page for the notion that water in the garden should serve three functions – reflection, movement, and sound. The garden already had still water in the reflecting pool in front of the temple. The fountain added sound and movement.

Before the fountain could be installed, a trench had to be dug to allow for the necessary piping and an area excavated to hold the fountain pool. Rosemary had inherited Arthur Turner, who had served as Linda Verey's head gardener and came with the house. He was getting on in years and was not someone Rosemary could easily command since he had run his own show for so many decades. While her mother-in-law was still alive, Rosemary decided that "Mr. Turner the Head Gardener and I must become good friends. So I approached him and said, 'which day would you like to meet me and discuss this week's work?' His answer was a shock. 'Mrs. Verey never interfered or questioned my work, so why should you?'"[8] They came to a polite truce and when Rosemary began to garden herself, he was left in charge of the vegetables on the other side of the farm lane, and Rosemary took responsibility for the pleasure or flower garden inside the wall.

Eventually Rosemary hired Arthur's brother-in-law, Fred Willis, who was even older than Arthur. Fred and his wife arrived at some point to assist with the developing flower borders and also to run the local post office-cum-small shop in the village. When the fountain arrived, Arthur Turner agreed to remove the turf but flatly refused to dig the trench. Fred, who was then in his seventies but a little more flexible, worked side by side with the indefatigable Rosemary to do the necessary digging. It proved a long and arduous task. Arthur did agree to wheel away the good soil as Rosemary and Fred laboriously dug it out since he could use it in his vegetable garden. Rosemary and Fred then installed the concrete lining for the fountain's pool, cementing it all in place and covering it with stone to make it look natural.

There being nothing like a deadline, the fountain was switched on and fortunately worked, just minutes before the garden opened to the public that year on June 4, 1972. More than three hundred people arrived that day. David was pleased that the garden "was looking immaculately tidy and very beautiful. Everyone was saying how perfect are the colour combinations and layout, etc. the laburnum walk, almost perfect, and fountain very entertaining."[9] Writing about the fountain for her short essay in *The Countryman* that year, Rosemary noted they built it because they needed a focal point. But in order to fit in with the character of the garden, she added, "It could not possibly be grand. That would be like wearing a tiara for tennis."[10] That year, Simon's fountain was featured on the cover of the National Gardens Scheme's Yellow Book, a listing of gardens in England and Wales open for charity.

Indeed it was so successful that Rosemary next asked him to carve a stone column that would be the focal point at the end of the laburnum walk, which ran parallel to the long walk from the temple to the new fountain. The following year, Simon created a handsome stone plinth that Rosemary presented to David for his sixtieth birthday. For Simon, she provided a quote from John Evelyn out of one of her antique garden books, and he carved the words "As no man can be miserable that is master of a Garden here; so will no man ever be happy who is not sure of a Garden hereafter. Where the first Adam fell the second rose." This plinth proved a perfect ending to the laburnum walk that would become an iconic image seen in countless photographs.

Simon became one of Rosemary's favorite protégés; she recommended him whenever she could to anyone she thought might hire him to enhance their own gardens with one of his creations. Among her most endearing traits was the very real pleasure she took in promoting her protégés. She pushed forward those who had performed well for her, and her recommendations became increasingly valuable as her own reputation grew. Her persistence and insistence that a particular person be hired made all the difference. Rosemary suggested Simon Verity to Diany Binny, the owner of Kiftsgate Court, a private garden adjacent to Hidcote Manor near Chipping Camden. Simon carved an enchanting garden seat at the end of a rose allée; it was the figure of a woman seated with her head leaning to one side, her arms clasped alongside her lap with the lap itself forming the seat of the chair. "Once she decided you were a good idea, that was it. You were on her list and you'd hear the amazing voice over the telephone ordering you to do this or that," Simon recalled.

Barnsley was fast becoming known in horticultural circles. Russell Page arrived and soon became a regular visitor. Rosemary always credited him with teaching her important lessons, first from his book *The Education of a Gardener*, which she had read early in her gardening life, and then from their friendship. He taught her important lessons about firm structure, the use of space, and above all "to use my eyes and imagination." She recalled him standing "on our lawn with his arms outstretched saying, 'This is where you must have a tree. Plant me here.' Our mulberry tree now flourishes there."[11]

It wasn't until Arthur Turner retired in 1975 that Rosemary

could finally take charge of the vegetable garden and turn her attentions to what would become her signature creation, her potager. "In those days you didn't get rid of old retainers . . . they worked until they dropped or retired."[12] Inspired by her visit to Villandry, a magnificent formal garden in France where she admired the interplay of planting beds shaped in the geometric patterns she so loved, Rosemary's genius was to borrow these ideas, with all their complexity and formality, and then to dramatically reduce the scale to fit the much smaller area of her own potager. She threw over the long-established tradition of planting vegetables in purely functional, straight rows, creating instead geometric shapes to serve as planting beds. She was sure a vegetable garden could be visually attractive as well as productive and she made this idea work in the confined area where Arthur Turner had himself grown vegetables. It was located outside the main garden within a low stone wall, next to the tennis court, just beyond the garden gate and across the farm lane.

In England, the walled garden was an integral part of every large garden; it was where vegetables and fruits for the household were grown, along with some flowers for cutting. "In the 1960s and 1970s walled gardens all over the country were turned into car parks, leased to commercial nurseries or simply allowed to decay." The word *potager* was the French word for a vegetable garden, "but it came to mean an ornamental kitchen garden thanks to Villandry."[13]

Rosemary's design called for a complex combination of narrow paths of brick and stone to define the patterns and shapes of the beds. Ever thrifty, Rosemary and Caroline Burgess scavenged for bricks and stones being tossed away on road construction sites. The paths they built formed many small planting areas. This appealed to Rosemary since these smaller growing beds allowed the working gardener easy reach for the necessary work as well as for easy picking later on. Caroline remembers that "it was all mathematically designed and worked out. We would do the 3–4–5 triangle in every corner. She'd work out how to make the circle and how to do this and how many bricks we had got to get." This formula of 3–4–5, based on the Golden Mean would have been familiar to Rosemary from her mathematical background and her knowledge of classical design. It is still used by carpenters as the way to achieve a true right angle. Rosemary used multiples of this basic formula to create the shapes in her potager, but ever the teacher, she quizzed Caroline on her multiplication tables as they worked. Although she drew the plans on squared paper and was careful about the right angles, Rosemary laid it out on the ground more by her discerning eye than by strict adherence to formulae or preconceived plans. She had learned that almost no growing area has the perfect symmetry of a paper plan; it always requires adjusting on site.

To provide the added interest of height, Rosemary espaliered apple trees into goblets, grew squash cascading from tall, curved metal hoops arching over a path, adding standard roses and other vertical accents. She produced wonderful combinations by mixing different colors and textures of vegetables: dark red-leafed lettuce interlacing swirls of green ones, leeks emerging among the cabbages. She allowed flowers to self-seed and intermingle throughout and edged the beds with low plantings of lavender or box, punctuated occasionally by box balls. On either side of the square enclosure, small teak chairs sat under homespun lattice arbors engulfed in vines, providing a shady resting spot for the weary gardener or admiring visitor.

Friends who came to stay shared the same experience of going out with Rosemary to the potager to pick things for their dinner. Her friend, David Farquharson would remember, "The potager – the kitchen garden – was the neatest and most beautiful and when I was staying there, before a meal, Rosemary would say go get some vegetables. We'd go across the lane and she would have a sharp knife in her hand and she would go round plucking little pieces of it. It was really a wonderful demonstration of how attractive a kitchen garden can be when you really laid it out as a garden."

More often visitors who were sent out alone to "pick things from the potager" found it a terrifying experience. Fearful of disrupting or destroying the beautiful, complex patterns of color, texture, and foliage, only the bravest succeeded in extracting the evening vegetables. Some preferred the more functional approach to growing vegetables in straight rows. Although Rosemary's friend and renowned garden designer, Penelope Hobhouse, thought the potager was a "miracle," she found it too artificial to her taste, preferring to grow vegetables in straight functional lines so she could pick a lettuce without worrying about spoiling the entire design.

Some time after Arthur Turner retired, Rosemary was fortunate in hiring a local lad, Andy Bailey, to come work in her garden right out of high school. It was his first job, he learned his craft from Rosemary, and his special interest was in the potager.[14] A bit later, his brother, Les, joined them and the two brothers remained a quiet force in the maintenance of the gardens for fifteen years. They also complemented each other, Andy being the mechanical type in charge of the vegetables and garden machines, and Les learning all the Latin names for the plants and concentrating on the flower borders.

Although Rosemary did not use the language of organic acolytes, her gardening practices were essentially organic in approach. She always insisted on the need for enriching the soil with manures and used her own homemade compost to pot up her plants. Cow manure was easily available, but she adopted her own ingenious methods involving her hens. Outside the garden, she kept chickens in a large pen, surrounded by a high wire fence. She'd throw into the pen all the kitchen scraps and all the cuttings from the garden, (excepting the really wicked weeds, like ground elder and convolvulus and poisonous plants like hellebores), and also corn. Whenever the chickens saw a wheelbarrow approaching, they would gather excitedly around the gate of their enclosure and immediately start pecking and scratching, competing for the best pieces. If the pen got very wet and a terrible mess ensued, she would add straw.

The chickens proceeded to scratch into all of that, adding their own chicken manure to the mix until the entire ground level rose over time. When the level of the run rose two feet or more, high enough for the chickens to flap out over the top, that was the signal for Rosemary's son Christopher Verey to arrive with his front-end loader, preferably on a frosty morning so the tractor wheels would not leave horrendous marks on the grass. He would scoop out the entire mess to use as compost in the garden, and after it aged a bit, the Bailey brothers would fling the stuff against a screen to break down the big, hard clumps, then add some lighter material such as perlite with a bit of slow release fertilizer. Mixed all together, it became her living compost heap.

Rosemary always emphasized the importance of feeding the soil, insisting, "You mustn't take more out of the soil than you put in." Good soil preparation and ongoing enrichment were essential. But simply enriching the planting hole was a bad idea. "People buy these plants and put them in the ground, and the plants don't know what hit them. It's like giving a nine-month-old baby roast beef and sausages. They're not happy."[15]

David was less interested in the hands-on aspect of the garden, and unlike the gregarious Rosemary, who adored an audience, he did not particularly enjoy the visitors who began appearing in increasing numbers. His daughter Veronica recalls him cutting hedges but doesn't remember him doing any other gardening at all.[16] To avoid the crowds, he created his own secret garden outside the hedges enclosing the main gardens where he could get away from people and avoid the crowds. He always had a refuge: first, retreating to the swimming pool behind the hedges, and when people started sticking their noses around the hedges too often, moving behind the summer house. He didn't require much, just a seat and a few fruit trees where he could relax and avoid the intrusion of strangers into his private world, his little escape, his own garden. Caroline Burgess observed, "There was nowhere else for him to go, other than to just stay in the house. Barnsley was inundated with people, because there's no real private part of the garden." While David was proud of their garden and Rosemary's showing it off, his own preference for privacy sharply contrasted with Rosemary's delight in her fans.

Continuing his own writings and faithfully maintaining a diary in the tradition of his family, he became chairman of a local publisher, Alan Sutton, which published his books, first *Cotswold Churches* (1976), then *The Diary of a Cotswold Parson* (1978), and finally *The Diary of a Victorian Squire* (1983). Simon Verity recounts, "David, I loved. He was maddeningly diffident but charming. He was very good looking but he had this awkward shyness that used to drive Rosemary demented. They had a strange relationship. She would bully him and he took it but he was very supportive of her."

His support was indispensable to Rosemary's success. It was David who took Rosemary on her first trip to the United States in 1978. While they were both invited to give talks to the North Carolina Fine Arts Society, Rosemary had second billing to David, who, regarded as an accomplished architectural historian, was to talk about historic churches. Rosemary's two talks were short and illustrated with slides; one was on "English Gardens Today" and the other on "Early Gardening Books." Traveling on the *Queen Elizabeth 2*, they were gone for several weeks, spending time with old friends in New York and then flying to Raleigh, North Carolina. It was the start of Rosemary's love affair with America.

David also introduced Rosemary to Alvilde Lees-Milne who would launch Rosemary on her first critically important book in 1980. David was close to Alvilde's husband, James Lees-Milne, who lived nearby at Alderley Grange, shared a mutual affinity for historic architecture and was another dedicated diarist. Lees-Milne was one of the founders of the National Trust created to preserve historic English architecture and David became chairman of the regional committee. He was also an intellectual and literary figure of some repute; the volumes of his autobiography are still read and admired.

Alvilde had created her own lovely small garden, very much in the style that Rosemary would emulate at Barnsley. Her first garden was at Alderley Grange, which she began in 1961; in 1975 she moved and gardened at Essex House as a tenant of the Duke of Beaufort on his Badminton estate. Both were very close to Barnsley. Rosemary thought Alvilde's gardens were perfect and that Alvilde was a "much better gardener than most of us. All is full and she has this feeling of joy using every patch to capacity. Things are tutored, tidy, but not studied." Alvilde used clipped box, hollies, and flowers in exuberant plantings, which Rosemary adopted. Caroline Burgess often went to Alvilde's to collect plants for propagation at Barnsley. Alvilde Lees-Milne was a strong partner for her early on. "She had a tremendous sense of style. And she made a wonderful garden in a similar style to Rosemary's, formal patterns and a very soft overlay. She was also a very formidable character, even more so than Rosemary," Stephen Lacey observed, describing Alvilde as "a much more frightening person. But I'm sure they must have greatly appreciated each other." Alvilde was also tough and could be extremely rude. The writer Anna Pavord mused that Alvilde and Rosemary together must have seemed like the "clash of the titans!"

Alvilde was far better known than Rosemary, both as a garden designer and as the wife of James Lees-Milne. She had been invited by Chatto and Windus to write the book that became *The Englishwoman's Garden* and she, in turn, enlisted Rosemary to help her with it. Conceived by the editor as a vehicle to introduce the gardens of fashionable English women, preferably either titled or at least upper class, forty women were asked to write a short piece about their garden, illustrated with a sketch of their house and color photographs. The book followed the general format of other titles that had recently been published and proved popular, one example being *The Englishwoman's Kitchen*.

The Englishwoman's Garden proved a considerable success, not only because of the occasional titled grande dame but more, in David Wheeler's words, because "They were writing about a very homely subject and were [breaking] down barriers of all kinds. People went off to see these gardens and these people were in their gardens, not just the head gardener in a stiff apron. These people had dirt under their fingernails. It was all rather wonderful."

The format was simple, requiring almost no writing from either Rosemary or Alvilde. All they had to do was to identify and invite women with attractive gardens to write a short essay, compile and edit the collection, and write a foreword. Rosemary's daughter Davina produced charming small drawings for each of the houses to introduce the essays. The quality of the photographs in this first book is rather poor, certainly not up to the standards of Rosemary's later books. But it was Rosemary's garden, not Alvilde's that was most prominently featured with a photograph of the laburnum walk on the cover and the frontispiece. Characteristically, Rosemary seized the moment and made it her own.

This also gave her an opportunity to hone one of her greatest skills, her ability to network. This impressive list of women with extraordinary gardens would all fill her address book; she would recommend protégés to them and reach out when she needed them. She had already met Sir Roy Strong, then head of the Victoria and Albert Museum in London. Because of her knowledge of English garden history, she served as an adviser to an exhibit he organized there in 1979. Strong believed this exhibit helped revive Gertrude Jekyll's reputation, which had been in eclipse, and put her back on the map. Never shy about calling upon people, Rosemary asked Roy Strong to write the foreword to *The English-woman's Garden* and he appears at once surprised and flattered by the invitation, writing, "It seems to me at once rather strange and immensely flattering that a mere man has been asked to write a foreword to this book, let alone a man who only discovered the art of gardening about six years ago."

Alvilde wrote the preface, but she gives credit to Rosemary, saying, "When this book was first suggested to me my immediate response was, 'No, it won't work.' How on earth, I thought, could a good book emerge, compiled mostly by amateur writers? However, albeit with misgivings, I agreed to go ahead. I asked Rosemary Verey if she would be willing to join me as co-editor. Fortunately for me she accepted since, without her patience, her industry, and above all her botanical knowledge, the book would never have become the worthwhile volume it is."

Although Alvilde gets first billing as co-editor and her name appears before Rosemary's, she did not write an essay about her own garden, but Rosemary wrote a five-page essay on Barnsley. Her essay is informed by history and her herbals, but the style is breezy, informal, and accessible. She engages the reader by admitting how difficult it was to get started, reveals her own mistakes, and conveys her enthusiasm. "The assurance that people had lived and gardened here for so long was a tremendous incentive for me to add my contribution. But, curiously, I knew I need not hurry, and I still have this feeling. Good 'bones' are important, so it is wise to go slowly and get your plan right before launching into a vital project. Now I love thinking out and creating a new incident. Then I felt totally bewildered and unable to start." After describing the stages of her own garden's development and acknowledging that "the vital impetus has always been my husband urging me on, expecting borders to be made in a flash and imagining I would know how to do it," she concludes with a modest "After all, I know I cannot make anything new, it has all been done before; but I can try to bring together all the best ideas passed on to me by present-day friends and old-fashioned writers and combine them with my own thoughts and so, I hope, create a garden which feels loved and longs to be walked in."

The Englishwoman's Garden was published in 1980. It was the first of eighteen books Rosemary would complete in her lifetime.

CHAPTER FIVE

The Books Begin
Early 1980s

More of a do'er than a writer.

S SOON AS *The Englishwoman's Garden* was out, Rosemary seized the moment and flew with David to the United States to promote it. This was her second trip to America, but this time Rosemary, not David, was the star attraction. She had her book to pitch and pitch it she did. She made the rounds of bookshops, signing books wherever she went. Since Barnsley was among the gardens featured in the book, she showed slides of it at every opportunity, promoting it as a mandatory destination for American visitors. Rosemary's career took off with this book. She was sixty-two.

When Alvilde Lees-Milne asked Rosemary to help her on *The Englishwoman's Garden* book, Alvilde probably had no idea how quickly Rosemary would take over. After all, she was the publisher's choice to produce the book and almost a decade older than Rosemary. She also had a formidable reputation, having been part of the social scene in France while married to her first husband, Viscount Chaplin, then divorcing to marry James Lees-Milne in 1951. Throughout both marriages, her affairs with women – including one with Vita Sackville-West – were discreet but known in certain circles, while James indulged in his preference for men. Over seventy by the time of the book, Alvilde no doubt needed

Rosemary's energetic support but was probably surprised how quickly Rosemary overshadowed her.

Rosemary loved being in the spotlight. This was her time to shine, and she was going to make the most of it. She had begun to taste success and some recognition through her magazine writings and Barnsley's growing reputation as a garden not to be missed. In her efforts to publicize the book, she worked hard to promote herself. It was her idea to travel to America to push the book and to pay for the trip herself. An often-published writer-friend, Anne de Courcy, asked, "Are your publishers sending you, because mine never sent me anywhere." Rosemary replied, "No, no, I'm paying for it myself. I think it's vital." She went. Alvilde didn't. Although quite formidable herself, Alvilde didn't have that drive. Drive, it was like Rosemary was on fire. Soon after the success of *The Englishwoman's Garden*, someone else approached Alvilde with an offer to co-author a book about English cottage gardens – without Rosemary. "Rosemary went ballistic. She was going to hang on to that with every breath. This was a tigress."[1]

The Englishwoman's Garden was a tremendous success. Before it appeared, there had been few, if any, large-format gardening books with beautiful color photography. By modern standards, the photographs seem uninspired and appear flat and dull. The book came out before high-quality reproduction of color photography became less expensive, so the photographs seem a bit washed out by today's standards. Nevertheless, they appealed to the public.

The book proved to be enormously popular, not only in England, but in America where an interest in gardening was beginning to burgeon and where the English garden was thought to be the epitome of good taste. Lynden Miller, a highly regarded American designer of public gardens, observed that "Americans were traveling to England, they were reading English garden books, they were beginning to go on those tours."

The timing was also ripe in England. Margaret Thatcher became Prime Minister in 1979 and England began finally to emerge from the hard times of the post-World War II era, moving to greater affluence across most levels of the population. Rosemary benefited from the shift; she later observed that what had once been the "provenance of the upper class [with their gardening staff] became the passion of the middle class."[2] The English had more discretionary, disposable funds available and began to return to their inherent interest in ornamental gardens. Another English garden writer, Stephen Lacey, recalled that in the "seventies, garden design really was in the doldrums. We were still in this slightly post-war gloom[with] ground cover, low-maintenance gardens. It was a total mess, no style in garden design at all. And then Rosemary sort of stepped in, reminding us of the great gardening heritage of the past, reconnecting us to that more glamorous gardening tradition. Everyone was all fired up again. Everyone was ready for gardening and had the appetite for it. She was there at the right time."

Shortly before the book appeared, Rosemary wrote a second article for *Country Life* in 1979. Based on her impressive library, the article concerned her old herbal books. Christopher Lloyd, himself a renowned horticulturist and contributor to *Country Life* with his own extraordinary garden at Great Dixter, took note of her article and sent Rosemary a letter congratulating her. He advised, "Be yourself in writing, Rosemary. You're a Queen Bee and positive. That's nothing to be ashamed of or to conceal."[3] Rosemary followed his wise advice and began short monthly essays for *Country Life* called "A Countrywoman's Notes," focused more on her observations of the countryside and natural world than on gardens. These short essays continued in almost unbroken succession until 1987. Eventually her daughter Davina Verey Wynne-Jones selected the best of these pieces and published them in a privately printed book in 1990 entitled *A Countrywoman's Year.*

With the success of *The Englishwoman's Garden*, Rosemary and Alvilde quickly turned to a sequel with *The Englishman's Garden* following the same format.[4] The foreword was written by the Marchioness of Salisbury. This time the preface was signed by both Alvilde and Rosemary.

Rosemary also undertook to write a serious book by herself, *The Scented Garden*. The idea for this book originated with Ethne Clarke, an American living in England who worked in book publishing and was just getting interested in gardening. When Ethne decided she wanted to make a scented garden at her first home in the south of London, she was frustrated when she was unable to find the right book to help her. She decided to sell the idea to a book packager and get one produced. Marshall Editions was interested and agreed to take this project on, with Ethne Clarke as the editor: the writer yet to be identified. Shortly thereafter, Rosemary appeared with her agent to complete the package.

Always enterprising, Rosemary had encountered Felicity Bryan when she came to see Rosemary's gardens after reading *The Englishwoman's Garden*. Learning that Felicity had begun to represent gardening authors after having served as gardening correspondent for the *Evening Standard*, Rosemary said, "I think I need an agent," and so she gained Felicity's invaluable help.

Ethne Clarke hadn't a clue who Rosemary Verey was and knew nothing about her first book. Innocently, Ethne asked Rosemary, "Do you have a garden?" And Rosemary said caus-

tically, "A little bit around the house."⁵ Despite this inauspi-
cious start, the two got on famously. Ethne had a very clear
plan for every spread in the book and contributed a great deal
to its writing. She and Rosemary quickly became friends, as
Ethne spent a great deal of time at Barnsley working on the
book. During the Christmas holidays, Rosemary invited Ethne
to join her and David at a party nearby hosted by Rosemary's
friend, Hardy Amies, dress designer to the Queen. They had
become great friends when Rosemary helped him with a bit
of advice and some planting in his garden. Ethne thought
David was a "charming man, very reticent and very quiet, re-
served and scholarly." She and David "trundled along behind
Rosemary who was at the head of the team into this room
full of people and Rosemary steaming through it. Everybody
knew Rosemary and Rosemary knew everybody and David
and I were just like little shrinking violets against the wall
watching Rosemary's progress through the room." Ethne saw
David as Rosemary's anchor; he kept her grounded.

Unlike *The Englishwoman's Garden*, this second book is
a substantive piece of writing, with far more text than pictures. *The Scented Garden* appeared in 1981 in both England and America; its subtitle was "Choosing, Growing and
Using the Plants that Bring Fragrance to Your Life, Home
and Table." The book focused on scented plants and how to
grow and use them in the garden. There are charming illustrations, mostly of the plants described, along with repro-
ductions of etchings and plates from historic books.
Interestingly, there are very few photographs.

In her introduction, Rosemary encourages the reader to
"explore the world of scents around you. You will be amazed
by its diversity. I do not believe that you can increase your
ability to smell, but you can certainly become increasingly
aware of scent. Some scents have truly to be discovered, as

some plants are 'fast' of their scent . . . they hold it until touched or even squeezed, while other plants are free with their scent, wafting it upon the air."[6]

With her deep admiration and knowledge of the early garden writers and herbalists, she quotes them extensively throughout the book. Noting her own appreciation of the early and intimate Tudor and Stuart gardens, full of flowers planted for their perfume, she described what she viewed as two unfortunate trends that pushed scented plants away. These were the "eighteenth-century landscape movement and the nineteenth-century Victorian vogue for bedding out and carpet bedding. The first caused the homely, scented blooms to be banished from beside the house to a concealed plot some distance away, so that they did not intrude upon the sweeping lawns and stately trees creating the carefully structured vista. The second did bring flowers back to the vicinity of the house, but garden owners attached far more importance to bright colours than to perfume." She credited William Robinson and Gertrude Jekyll as the Edwardian gardeners who encouraged people to fill their plots with hardy, sweetly scented plants.

The book is full of practical advice, such as "Plants that release their perfume easily should be planted so the prevailing wind will bring the scent to you." In discussing scents in the evening, "as the light fades and the warmth of the day's sun enhances the floral perfumes," she says, "This benison is something for which all gardeners who are confined during the day to city offices should be grateful, for if flowers were fragrant only by day, the weary worker would miss so much."

The chapters are divided into plant types; the first is on roses, then annuals, biennials, and perennials, next bulbs, corms, and tubers, then one on herbs, including detailed illustrations of her beloved patterns as well as useful recipes, followed by shrubs, trees, and climbers, and finally fragrant exotica. Each chapter starts out with a list of the plants to grow, and the book ends with a long, alphabetical list of recommended plants.

Her books were setting Rosemary apart from the countless other country women with nice houses and lovely gardens. This book was particularly important. Unlike her books with Alvilde, she wrote this one herself, and it was not merely a collection of essays written by others, it was a substantive work on an interesting subject, well written and accessible to the gardening public. It drew upon her interest in garden history while combining her practical advice about how to do it, gleaned from her hands-on experience. It also helped to have a superb editor in Ethne Clarke.

The Scented Garden was well received by the reviewers and ranked fourth on the *London Times* list of best-selling books in November 1981. In a *Daily Telegraph* interview, Rosemary claimed she wrote the book in only five months, declaring she was "much more of a do'er than a writer." The interviewer described her as "silver-haired and suitably weather beaten, the epitome of the English woman gardener – an integral part of that redoubtable kind of women who are as cultivated as their garden."[7] *Country Life* proclaimed "by no means should the chintzy layout of this book damn it as another coffee table production. ... [It was full of the] author's gardening experiences – all manner of anecdotes and histories that a well versed patrician gardener might recount to a garden-struck novice. It was absorbing, scholarly and delightful, made practical by hints of how best to grow the scented plants."[8]

Once *The Scented Garden* was finished but before it was out, the Vereys traveled to America for a third time in the fall of 1981, leaving Barnsley behind for five weeks in the capable hands of Caroline Burgess. Frank Cabot, the American gardenmaker extraordinaire and philanthropist, had invited Rosemary to give a lecture at Wave Hill in New York. Formerly a private twenty-eight-acre estate overlooking the Hudson River with the cliffs of the New Jersey Palisades beyond it, Wave Hill had been given to the City of New York for the benefit of the public by the family of Frank Cabot's wife, Anne. It was fast becoming one of the most artistic and adventurous gardens in the United States under the horticultural leadership of Marco Polo Stufano. Frank Cabot remembers that Rosemary spoke with "great vigor and wonderfully, captivating everybody. She had this wonderful radiant personality and everybody loved her. She was very outgoing and immediately you were her friend no matter who you were. . . . She was the only English person I know who came to America and then ended up knowing and having more friends in America than any American had."

Her talk at Wave Hill was very well received, even though it presented quite a challenge. The event was Wave Hill's annual Gardener's Fair and Picnic, which attracted supporters of Wave Hill along with many enthusiastic gardeners, who came to meet and greet each other, buy the rare plants offered for sale, and to party. Rosemary spoke after her audience had enjoyed their dinner and had a few too many drinks; it was late and they were tired. Her talk was on "Great English Women Gardeners since 1700," drawing again on her interest in gardening history. But despite the late hour and the scholarly topic, her vivacious personality and obvious knowledge won them over. She enjoyed herself enormously and she particularly enjoyed being in the company of admiring Americans.

Rosemary took advantage of every opportunity to connect

with influential people in American horticultural circles. As an early disciple and then a close friend of the garden designer, Russell Page, she went with him to see his creations at Pepsico, the corporate headquarters of the Pepsi-Cola Company in Westchester, New York. She went to Philadelphia to meet Jane Pepper, then President of the Pennsylvania Horticultural Society, and on to see the heads of Longwood Gardens and Winterthur, two renowned du Pont institutions near Wilmington, Delaware. Everywhere she went, she added the names of Americans she met on the way to her growing address book. Although in her later extensive travels she would come to know more different parts of America than most Americans, in 1981 she was just beginning to learn about the place. In one note to herself she records her discovery that "New Jersey is a State."[9]

Rosemary charmed her audiences and built her growing fan club. Just as she was a quick study of plants, she was equally adept at sizing up the people she met. She issued liberal invitations to come visit Barnsley. One example of her incredible networking and focused follow-up grew out of her visit to Wilmington where she met Bill and Nancy Frederick. The Fredericks had their own boutique nursery and personal garden in the beautiful Brandywine Valley. Bill also served on the boards of Winterthur and Longwood Gardens. When he told her about his interest in English botanical watercolors, particularly those by Margaret Waterfield, she didn't forget his interest. Soon thereafter she appealed to her readers in one of her monthly *Country Life* articles. "A thought has been brewing in my mind put there by one of the Directors of Longwood Gardens near Philadelphia. He asked me if I knew where he could find water colours of late Victorians and Edwardians, especially Margaret Waterfield."[10] She then wrote to the Fredericks conveying all the responses. Not surprisingly, the

Fredericks quickly went to England to follow up and spent several weeks buying Waterfields for their collection while establishing a lifelong friendship with Rosemary.

David traveled alongside, meeting people in horticultural circles. Frank Cabot thought David "was quiet and scholarly. . . . Just a charming gentleman who was a quiet mate for Rosemary." However, David certainly held his own. Bill Frederick remembered him "as an architectural historian and we adored him. He had a great passion for what he was doing, but perhaps he was not always disciplined about the management of funds. Rosemary was much more practical but I think she totally appreciated his enthusiasm and his whims."

Following her own rules, Rosemary was always learning; she never walked through any garden without a notebook in hand to jot down observations, plants, and ideas. With her keen mind, sharp eye, and excellent memory, coupled with her unfailing practice of taking notes wherever she went, Rosemary carried away new plants and design ideas from the many great gardens she visited and the accomplished gardeners she met to enrich her own education.

Unlike many English gardeners, she was not dismissive of the wonderful American gardens she encountered. On this trip, she and David went to California where she visited the impressive gardens at Filoli. It was the first time she had ever seen a knot garden where "the interlacing 'threads' had been clipped to give the impression that they go over and under one another. I had never seen this done in England, so on coming home we got busy with clippers and started to shape the intersections of our knots to convey this impression. The patterns were immediately given new life and a rhythm of which I feel sure the Elizabethans were aware, although I have never found it conveyed in old books."[11]

Throughout her trip in America, Rosemary promoted

Barnsley and encouraged people to come. She would even generously invite people she had just met. Lynden Miller, who would later become an important and well-known designer of public American gardens, met Rosemary on that 1981 trip when Rosemary spoke at Wave Hill. When Lynden lived in England in the late 1970s with her husband, Leigh Miller, she hired the famous garden designer, Lanning Roper, to work on her own small London garden. She also took courses at Chelsea & Westminster College in London and, after moving back to New York, at the New York Botanical Garden. At this first meeting, Lynden mentioned to Rosemary that she wanted to spend some time studying the gardens at Hidcote. Rosemary interrupted "in her very abrupt way,. . . [and said] 'Let me see your hands.' So I brought my hands out and of course they were dirty. And she said, 'Okay, you are a gardener . . . so would you like to come and stay at my house while you study Hidcote?' I was overwhelmed. I had never met her before." Although Rosemary was generous in her invitations to come and stay, that was only after she decided the person being invited was genuinely interested in the garden.

Although she could not have known Lynden would go on to become a leading light in American horticultural circles, her invitation was genuine, and Lynden's stay at Barnsley was memorable. She made the short trip back and forth to nearby Hidcote to study the famous gardens there, and also got to know Barnsley intimately. David "was darling to me. He was just the sweetest thing. And I would get up at 5:30 A.M. and there would be photographers out there already." Rosemary had invited the Lees-Milnes to dinner, and Lynden sat between Alvilde and Rosemary. She found Alvilde "terrifying. You are talking two incredible powerhouses. I mean you could feel the sparks fly, although they were friends." Lynden was just one of many Americans who took up Rosemary's invitation to visit Barnsley, often to stay there. And the visits paid off; they went back to spread the word that Barnsley was a "must see" for Americans making the rounds of English gardens.

Part of Rosemary's appeal, particularly in America, was due to her style. Americans always love a British accent and hers was perfection. Just the right hint of upper class but without a trace of condescension, often graced with an easy laugh. She paid attention to her clothes, dressing conservatively, always in a skirt or dress, but in attractive colors. If black was the chic color for sophisticated New Yorkers, black was not for Rosemary. Multi-stranded pearls graced her neck, below her carefully coiffed white hair, and there would always be something blue to set off her lively eyes. Lynden thought, "She was theatre wasn't she? I mean the hat and the flowered dresses and the beautiful voice and the acid wit. I mean Rosemary was not a sweet little thing. She was a real person, a real character." Sir Roy Strong summed it up. "She did fulfill a certain image, didn't she? I mean she had that absolute English lady of the manor [style]."

What was not evident to an outside observer was that David was seriously ill. He had been diagnosed with prostate cancer. After they returned home, his doctor advised that his condition was treatable but that he would face a difficult operation and prolonged treatment. Although her public face was completely stiff upper lip, privately Rosemary admonished herself in her diary, "Must not be too depressed," with triple underlinings.[12] The rest of Rosemary's diary that month is silent about his condition, devoted entirely to the garden and garden visitors. If not entirely in denial, both Vereys would maintain their privacy, self-discipline, and stoicism. Rosemary plunged into her work, her writing, and the garden, while David accepted the Lord Lieutenant's appointment to serve as one of the Deputy Lieutenants of Gloucestershire, another honorific role representing the Crown and dating back to the sixteenth century. There would be no more trips for Rosemary to America for the rest of David's life.

TOP: *The Winter Walk inside the 1770 garden wall, parallel to the lime allée and Laburnum Walk with Simon Verity's stone obelisks.*

ABOVE: *The Laburnum Walk.*

BELOW: *Barnsley House seen across red poppies in the parterre beds.*

LEFT: *Barnsley House with Irish yew lining the stepping stone walk planted with rock roses.*

BELOW: *The Gothick Summer House.*

BOTTOM: *The Temple David Verey brought to Barnsley House from Fairford Park.*

TOP: *The Knot Garden in front of the verandah in early days.*

ABOVE: *The Knot Garden touched by frost.*

LEFT: *The Herb Garden added to one of the parterres, seen from an upstairs window at Barnsley House.*

ABOVE: *An example of planting patterns in the Potager.*

BELOW: *Arches add height to the Potager while supporting a combination of flowers and vegetables, including sunflowers, rudbeckias, runner beans, and squash.*

David's Death;
Garden Design Work Begins
Early 1980s

*I just kind of felt shattered by it all, . . . but I knew I had to
go on. You had to brace yourself and say get on with it.*

OSEMARY'S GROWING reputation came
principally from her writings and from the
enthusiasm of visitors to her own maturing
gardens at Barnsley. In both arenas, she generously offered advice and shared her knowledge. What began as friendly, free advice to friends and
neighbors eventually led to a paid profession: a garden
designer for clients.

Rosemary's early garden design work was in England,
although she did send a small design to Canada for the Mon-
treal International Floralies in 1980. Several other important British organizations, including the Royal Horticultural
Society, had first been asked to create a garden for this event
but all had declined. The president of the Royal Rose Society,
unhappy at the lack of British representation, undertook to
remedy the situation by enlisting sponsors and contributors.
He approached Rosemary in December and she whipped
together a plan for a butterfly, bee, and herb garden that
appeared the following May. Rosemary was delighted by the
review that called it "an absolute jewel."[1]

Having inherited an Elizabethan house in 1980, Karen

and James Lowther asked Rosemary to advise them on their garden at Holdenby House in Northamptonshire. They turned to her because of her deep knowledge of garden history. She said, "My brief was twofold. I was to use only plants that were grown in England before 1580, and I was to make the garden as interesting and colourful as possible during the months from April until the end of September when the house and grounds were open to the public. This is where the old writers were invaluable."[2] This proved the perfect project for Rosemary; the hedges and shapes of the beds were already in place. She would change the plantings. She enjoyed the research and concluded, "History should always go hand in hand with artistic vision when old gardens are being brought back to life." She fantasized about walking through the garden with the original owner, Sir Christopher Hatton, Lord Chancellor to Queen Elizabeth I, and "learning more about the sixteenth century."

Other clients were neighbors. One was Robert Cooper, who had acquired a grand country estate with extensive grounds graced by the lovely River Coln in the village of Ablington where Rosemary and David had first lived at Hinton House. Rosemary helped him with the design of one of the many formal gardens he was establishing there, but her principal contribution was in the selection of plants, particularly which clematis and roses to grow on pergolas in a walled garden. She also helped Mr. and Mrs. Rupert Watson who lived in nearby Winson. None of these represented major jobs, just advice, perhaps a drawing or plant list for a border here or there.

Her first "royal" client was Princess Michael of Kent, who had bought a country home, Nether Lypiatt Manor, in Gloucestershire in 1981 not far from Barnsley. Her husband, Prince Michael, was a grandson of King George V and a cousin to the Queen. Princess Michael, like Rosemary, was keen about horses and a passionate gardener herself. She first met Rosemary as part of the "local gentry."[3] Initially, Rosemary was "just a friend, terribly helpful. She was free with advice and she was a great friend. She was a chum." Over friendly dinners, Rosemary provided her with ideas but never submitted a bill. Eventually Princess Michael commissioned her to design a circular garden at Nether Lypiatt and later an herb garden. "When I commissioned her to do something, that was different." This time Rosemary was paid for her work.

Princess Michael enjoyed Rosemary. She was "ebullient. Effervescent! Wonderfully energetic . . . and smart." Rosemary's "smart" ideas were also practical, drawn from years of direct, hands-on experience. As an example, she instructed Princess Michael's gardeners to place a liner underneath the gravel paths to prevent the weeds from growing through. Then she suggested they edge the lawns with metal to avoid the labor-intensive clipping and edging that would otherwise be necessary to keep things looking crisp. She realized that continued edging would eventually erode the shapes of the beds, although she didn't follow this good advice herself. Her own gardeners were constantly manually edging the Barnsley borders. Probably the expense of metal edgings put her off, or possibly she preferred the softer look of the lawn against earth. More often, rather than providing formal designs for Nether Lypiatt, Rosemary and Princess Michael traded ideas and suggestions about plants and garden improvements, much like any two friends and neighbors.

Another of Rosemary's first serious paying clients happened to be American. Arthur Reynolds and his wife, Catherine, had moved from the United States to London to pursue Arthur's career in finance. Because Catherine enjoyed riding and they both wanted a weekend country escape, they bought a cottage descriptively called The Little House in the village of Barnsley, just a few hundred yards down the main road from Rosemary's driveway. They met at the village church where both Rosemary and David were pillars of the congregation. Rosemary began to invite them home for tea or lunch after services, when she and Catherine discussed their shared love of horses. Arthur viewed the Vereys as part of the local aristocracy, or "squirearchy" as he called it.

He identified four main local characters: Christopher Wykeham-Musgrave, the last of a distinguished family who had inherited and then sold the imposing manor house in Barnsley Park; John Russell, the local farmer; Lord Faringdon, who had acquired and lived in Barnsley Park; and David Verey. At least such was Arthur's perception of the town's leading citizens, but as an American outsider, Arthur could never be entirely certain he fully understood the subtleties of the British class system.

When the Reynolds settled in and became interested in creating a garden around The Little House, it was natural to turn to Rosemary for advice, both as a neighbor and expert. Just as Rosemary had done when she began her Wilderness, the Reynolds, like many beginning gardeners, turned to experienced neighbors to find out what would grow well in their location. The Reynolds project provided Rosemary with her first opportunity to design an entire garden. She became deeply engaged in what was to become a charming garden, intimately tied to the house on a relatively small parcel of land.

At first, she concentrated on the front of the house, an area that faced the main road behind an existing beech hedge shielding the house from the village traffic. For this long, shady, narrow space, only ten feet wide, she produced a classic Rosemary Verey design. Clipped balls of box lined the path planted with narrow borders of flowering plants on either side. The path led to a larger square space beyond on the south side of the house, overlooked from the drawing room windows of the house. Rosemary often quoted Gertrude Jekyll, saying, "The garden should curtsey to the house," just as her own garden outside her drawing room at Barnsley had done. She meant that the garden should not only relate well to life within the house, both functionally and visually, but it should be compatible with its architecture.

In the center of the Reynolds' square garden area, she created four square, box-edged parterres, each divided by diagonals of box creating diamond-shaped small beds for seasonal plantings. The center of each parterre had a standard box ball for height. Looking out from the house, the evergreen outlines were visible in all seasons. To one side, she had Simon Verity carve a wall fountain to splash into a long pool for sound and movement. And to create a frame for all of this, she added pleached trees or what she called "hedges on stilts" to give "a feeling of structure without being too wall-like and confining."[4] Rather than use traditional limes or hornbeams, she chose *Sorbus aria lutescens* for the beauty of their silvery blue leaves. That was quite an unusual use of that particular tree. One of her talented protégés, Tim Rees, thought this was quite adventurous and copied the idea subsequently.

No doubt inspired by the potager Rosemary was developing at Barnsley, the Reynolds next asked for a vegetable garden just up the hill beyond the more formal area adjacent to the house. In her potager, Rosemary had been training apple trees into goblet shapes, tying them onto tall hoops and learning the proper pruning techniques. She adapted this idea for the Reynolds, but instead of goblets, she designed a charming row of tall arches above the central path and planted apple trees alongside to be trained to cover each arch. Aware that without proper pruning, these apples would only bloom along the top of each arch, Rosemary brought in a particularly skillful man who knew how to prune the apple trees to insure their blooms would cover the entire arch, creating a perfect semi-circle of leaf and blossom. The composition was completely entrancing.

Being Americans, the Reynolds brought some new ideas to the enterprise. Arthur decided to install lights. He loved the garden and he wanted to be able to see it even after dark, especially in the long, dark days of the English winter. "No one else had this idea of lighting up trees. That was considered peculiarly American. . . . I was about to say vulgarly American." When Arthur met the great garden designer Sir Geoffrey Jellicoe at some event, Jellicoe "launched into this diatribe. . . . If God wanted us to see trees at night under artificial lights. . ." But unlike Jellicoe, Rosemary was open to new ideas. The lights were installed to the Reynolds' delight. By now, garden lighting is commonplace.

Working in close collaboration with the Reynolds, taking into account their needs and taste, Rosemary kept up a lengthy correspondence even when they were away in London. Lists of plant suggestions that Catherine had clipped out of magazines or catalogues, replies, and other lists of plants from Rosemary flew back and forth. Catherine had strong views of her own, particularly regarding color. One such interchange produced a memorable outcome. When Catherine complained about a lavatera Rosemary had planted in one corner of The Little House, finding it much too magenta, too strident for the other plants of the border, Rosemary listened. Shortly thereafter, while driving through the countryside, her keen eye spotted a lavatera growing near the edge of the road, flowering a lovely pale silvery pink,

rather than the usual brighter tones. Out like a flash, Rosemary had cuttings in hand to take back to Barnsley to prop-
agate. The plant, now known as *Lavatera Barnsley*, is the
famous result.

Although Rosemary was open to Catherine's views, she
had strong views of her own. When Arthur Reynolds asked
if she would plant some aubrietia along the walls in front of
The Little House, she recoiled. Rosemary had "her own cat-
alogue of U and non-U plants," U being the popular short-
hand for "upperclass." She clearly regarded the commonplace
aubrietia as a non-U plant. Her reply, "I don't know how to
grow aubrietia," reflected her opinion, indicating that all dis-
cussion on the subject was at an end.

While Rosemary could design a garden for the Reynolds,
she was not up to installing the necessary structures, stone
walls, and paving. For this and many later assignments,
Rosemary called upon able assistance from John Hill. John
Hill and Rosemary first met in the late 1970s. John was a
friend of Rosemary's son, Charles, through their mutual in-
volvement in a spiritual movement called Beshara. Founded
in Scotland in 1973, Beshara promoted the search for greater
self-knowledge and understanding of one's relationship to
the rest of the universe through meditation and study. John
was working as a head gardener on a large estate at nearby
Sherborne when Charles urged John to come to Barnsley to
meet his mother. Eventually, John set up his own nursery at
Sherbourne, becoming an important partner in Rosemary's
garden design work, providing the heavy lifting required to
install the hardscape, and planting the large trees or shrubs
called for by Rosemary's designs.

John remembers their first meeting because as they
walked around the garden, he violated one of her basic rules.
"I remember the first time walking around the garden with

her, looking around [with Rosemary reeling off] plant name after plant name after plant name, which I wasn't bad at, but she had quite a few." John grew a little bored and gazed down at his feet. When she caught him not paying attention to her, she said sternly, "'and that's grass!' Put me in my place right there. Not listening."

Even though Rosemary was extremely knowledgeable and created a charming garden for the Reynolds, Arthur believes that she was deeply insecure, even though she didn't show it. After all, she didn't even have a basic university degree, never mind any formal horticultural credentials. She seemed to think of herself as in disguise, always worried about being found out by the real professionals and dismissed as an amateur. Perhaps this insecurity is what drove her to work so hard and become so good at it. But these were still quite early days.

A Canadian couple, Galen and Hilary Weston, came to Rosemary in the early 1980s to ask for her help with their gardens at Fort Belvedere, part of Windsor Great Park. The Fort had been built in 1750 and was best known as the former country home of King Edward VIII, the place where he had abdicated the throne to marry Wallis Simpson. Galen Weston was the head of the vast Weston enterprises that included chains of food stores and other corporate holdings in Canada, England, and America. The garden was truly in a fort, up among the crenellated battlements.

Rosemary arrived to re-plant a series of borders lining the walls of the battlements. Hilary Weston remembers Rosemary directing the gardeners to remove all the roses, which had become leggy. When Hilary resisted, since the roses had been there forever, Rosemary conceded but commanded, "Right, we'll cut them right back to the core, right down to the ground." To her credit, Rosemary admitted, "This is where I made an error. The climbing roses and clematis had become leggy enough to top the wall, and I suggested that they should all be severely cut back. Too late I realized that they had been allowed to behave like this so that they would flower through the crenellations on top of the wall and so be seen from the house. Eventually all was well."[5] The roses finally did grow back but it took quite a long time for them to fully recover.

Hilary, then a young woman in her thirties, found Rosemary delightful company, a wonderful mentor, and an inspiring role model. She thought the evolution of Rosemary's life from wife and mother to professional over the decades was an example to emulate. They worked together on ideas for Fort Belvedere over many more years. Hilary, who later became the Lieutenant Governor of Ontario, took particular encouragement from the fact that Rosemary "came to [gardening and fame] very late."

Hilary thought Rosemary was a wonderful plantswoman and that she taught her a lot about gardening. "I learned at her feet, if you will. And we had a lot of fun." After a day of working in the garden, and a break for lunch, they would return to the house around four or five o'clock. When Hilary offered a cup of tea, Rosemary always said, "No thank you, Darling, but how about a glass of sherry?" So they would sit down and have quite a few glasses of sherry. Despite the difference in their ages, Hilary found Rosemary "lively, clever and really, really good company." Galen Weston generally joined them for the conversation and the sherry.

More than a client, Hilary felt their relationship became "just a friendship. I think she was like that with most of the people that she worked with. She just had such an engaging personality that you immediately found that you were on the same page and then her actual drawings and her garden plans were very easy to read. She didn't pontificate about

gardening *per se*, she just was rooted in her world of gardening and she was generous to a fault in terms of sharing her
knowledge."

Rosemary's borders remain along the battlements at Fort
Belvedere, and because it is over 120 yards long, she created
large swathes of plants in a beautiful blending of color and
texture, especially silvers, grays, and pinks. The plantings
continue to be reworked and renewed by the current, highly
regarded designer, Tom Stuart-Smith – who advises the
Westons now – but Rosemary's basic structures and overall
design, along with her work on the rose garden, survive.

Because so much important work had been done by Russell Page at Longleat House, Rosemary was particularly
pleased when the Marquess and Marchioness of Bath asked
her to do a new planting plan for two long herbaceous borders there. The Marchioness was herself an accomplished
gardener and decided she wanted one section planted in
Rosemary's preferred palette of cool blues, mauves, pinks
and whites, the other planted in hot colors. Much of Rosemary's work was done on the site, extracting existing plants
to either toss or use again and adding new ones. Although
she hoped to be able to do more at Longleat, her assignment
there was limited.

Even as her garden design work expanded, Rosemary continued to produce books. Instead of collaborating with Alvilde,
she co-authored *The American Woman's Garden* with Ellen
Samuels.[6] It seems likely that Alvilde and Rosemary finally
had a falling out although Rosemary never said so. They certainly ended their collaboration. Alvilde came out with a
book called *The Englishwoman's House* just as Rosemary
published *The American Woman's Garden*.

Ellen, a wealthy American who had been developing her

own gardens on the site of an imposing 1920s estate on a small island off the coast of Long Island, thrust herself forward for the job. Ellen was an unlikely partner for Rosemary. A large, aggressive woman, married to a successful Texan who had made his fortune in the coal industry, Ellen lived in a large townhouse in Manhattan and spent weekends at her estate. Socially ambitious, she joined the horticulture committee at Wave Hill, and after hearing Rosemary speak there, she went to England to get to know Rosemary better. She parlayed their acquaintance into persuading Rosemary to allow her to co-author the book. Certainly, it made sense to have an American co-author a book about American gardens, someone who was on the ground and could find the best gardens to include, travel to vet each candidate, and deal with each woman asked to write an essay.

Rosemary dedicated this book to "My husband, David Verey, who shared my journeys to the United States." The preface was written by both authors, with Rosemary's name coming first. Ellen did most of the legwork for the book, but both editors benefited from Rosemary's wide and growing network of American horticultural connections and friends.[7]

The American Woman's Garden had an instant and obvious appeal to Americans. The book featured beautiful American gardens at a time when Americans had something of an inferiority complex, viewing English gardens as the apogee of the art, especially the art of perennial borders and flower gardens. Here was a book that showcased American gardens selected as worthy by a recognized English authority who was fast becoming the most famous English garden personality in America. By featuring American gardens, large and small, grand and modest, the book not only acknowledged that there were many marvelous American gardens in eighteen states, but also validated the aspirations of the many Americans who wanted to create them. The book gave Rosemary a tremendous boost with her growing numbers of American fans.

Perhaps because she was English, and doubtless because there were fewer American competitors on the scene, Rosemary's star seemed to burn brighter in America than in England. In England, she had to emerge from the pack and move beyond her earlier, conventional upper-class life as wife and mother. She had to compete in a crowded scene of serious gardeners and overcome the views of her countrymen who too easily could stereotype her. America was great for her.

After his own seventieth birthday celebration and both as a Christmas and birthday present for Rosemary in December of 1983, David presented Rosemary with a beautiful, red leather-bound book entitled *This is Our Garden*. It is a scrapbook full of clippings from newspapers and magazines about Barnsley from England, Germany, France, and America, along with many photographs. Garden figures of renown are prominently featured, either in the photographs or in articles written about Barnsley, including Peter Coats, an acclaimed garden designer himself who had become a close friend and frequent visitor. Russell Page, Sir Roy Strong, and the great plants couple, Valerie Finnis and Sir David Scott, were among the other gardening celebrities. There were also mementos from their travels to America together.

In the book is an article from *Cotswold Life*,[8] an interview with David about his own recent book, *The Diary of a Victorian Squire*, then out in a successful second edition. Noting that David had begun as an aspiring architect but, after his stint in the Army as a Captain in the Royal Fusiliers, wasn't happy about standing at a drawing board for exactly the same salary his wife paid her gardener, the article quotes him as saying with disarming candor, "'I regard myself as a failed architect because I have never practiced the profession." But the article ranks him as an eminent architectural historian. Having had such difficulty in passing his architectural qualifying exams as a young man or holding on to his first architectural job, one has to wonder if David really did regard himself with some regret as a failed architect, notwithstanding his success as an architectural historian.

In putting together the materials for this scrapbook, David unearthed some of the original designs for the garden. Rosemary's literary agent, Felicity Bryan, came to lunch around this time to encourage Rosemary to write a book about the making of the garden. When Rosemary stepped out of the room to get dessert, David said to Felicity, "It's important we assemble all this stuff now, for I am likely to die in a few months." Felicity still remembers his calm face and expressed her deep admiration for them both, "carrying on as if life were quite normal."

Rosemary was never as faithful or thorough a diarist as David, often chiding herself in her own diary for her failure to keep up to date. She was far more insistent about the daily entries she and her gardeners entered in the garden workbook, where they would list the chores done each day. She used these books for reference year to year to confirm what needed to be done by which date. However, in her personal diary on October 5, 1983, she optimistically noted that, "David is definitely better. Looks less fragile and has more energy."[9] But by that November, just before David gave her the beautiful scrapbook, she wrote simply, "David not feeling too well."

Most of Rosemary's diary entries reveal very little about her feelings or David's deteriorating condition as he struggled with cancer. Her daughter Veronica observed, "She was the generation she was. She was so stiff upper lip she had absolutely no way of talking about her own feelings and she never, to my knowledge, ever did so."

In 1984, Rosemary's book *Classic Garden Design* appeared, written solely by her. Like *The Scented Garden*, this is a substantive piece of writing, drawing upon her knowledge of garden history and her outstanding library of old garden books. Its subtitle is "How to Adapt and Recreate Garden Features of the Past." The writing is clear and accessible, while at the same time evidencing her deep knowledge of the subject as well as offering practical advice. She had used classical garden design and ideas at Barnsley, but scaled them down to fit into her own relatively small garden space. In the book, she seeks to encourage others to do the same, writing in the preface, "My intention in writing this book has been to provide an introduction to garden history by bringing the subject alive, and by looking at the history of different parts of the garden to show how these can be rich sources of ideas."

Eleven chapters cover details from paths, alleys, and walks through her favorite knot and herb gardens. Illustrations include color as well as black-and-white photographs along with sketches of how to lay out a proper knot garden with pegs and string. It is significant that she includes examples of American gardens. A reading list of books grouped by century, starting in the sixteenth and going through the nineteenth, is provided at the end of the book. She acknowledges that the book is "not an encyclopædia of gardening knowledge. There are no rules showing how gardens must be made, but there are examples which I hope will show what can be done." The book is dedicated to David "who moved a 1770 temple from Fairford Park thus creating a focus of great happiness in our garden."

Just as the stars were aligning for Rosemary, David's health deteriorated, and he died on May 3, 1984. He was buried in the churchyard at Barnsley, where other family graves are nearby. Simon Verity carved the beautiful stone roping along the edges of his stone, as well as the inscription and a small cross.[10] Rosemary recalled, "I just kind of felt shattered by it all. It somehow knocks you on the head in any form of creativity but I knew I had to go on. You had to brace yourself and say get on with it. I remember walking around the garden. It was beautiful. I hoped he hadn't gone too far away to enjoy it."[11] She was now entirely alone.

After David's Death
Mid-1980s

Since his death, I have been free to be my own person,
to go off anywhere I want.

ROSEMARY WAS devastated by David's death. They had been married for forty-five years, and except for the war years, David had been the head of the family and the force behind their Barnsley garden. Rosemary had cooked and provided lunch for David every day of their married life, other than the days when he was away during the war or was traveling to research historic buildings and churches. It is too simple to say his absence liberated Rosemary to devote even more energy to her public life. After having produced a book a year since her first book with Alvilde in 1980, there were no more books for the next three years.

On May 5, 1984, two days after he died, there was a church service in Barnsley. A subsequent service took place on June 1 in Gloucester Cathedral. One obituary states, after outlining his Army and Ministry of Housing careers, "It's as an architectural historian that he will be remembered ... for his *Shell Guide to Gloucestershire* (1952) and five other counties and two Gloucestershire volumes (1970) of Pevsner's Buildings of England. By several critics Verey's contributions were accounted the best of this remarkable series. ... Meticulous as to facts, his pen was always light, fluent and dryly humorous. In later years his interest was the Arlington Mill in Bibury when others had abandoned it, making it into a popular country museum and the beautiful garden at Barnsley. Slight, frail, dark, a trifle austere and touchingly diffident, he had the striking countenance of some medieval monk. Although the most courteous and affable of hosts, there clung to him an indefinable aura of asceticism and even sanctity."[1]

The family finances had been entirely David's domain. After his death, Rosemary was suddenly forced to take charge. David had been oblivious to matters of money, and he left things in disarray. Arthur Reynolds, Rosemary's friend, neighbor, and garden design client at The Little House, stepped in to help her cope. Even though Rosemary preferred keeping her concerns private, she had no experience in managing the family's money and was unhappily surprised to find herself with serious financial concerns and extensive debt.

In going through David's papers with Rosemary, Arthur found decades of bank statements that had never been opened. During their marriage, David hadn't involved Rosemary and had a somewhat cavalier attitude toward money. He relied on his bank manager to handle his bills and was frequently in overdraft in his account. When the overdraft grew large enough or too long outstanding to cause his banker to press him, he would sell some more land to cover the shortfall. But after David's death, the local bank manager was no longer as kind or patient as he had been with David. When Arthur asked her how she dealt with one particular tongue-lashing from the banker, Rosemary bravely replied, "I just laughed at him."

Making money then became an important part of Rosemary's motivation. She talked openly about her concerns to Arthur Reynolds and other close friends, particularly her sense of responsibility to help support her children and grandchildren. None of her four children had married wealthy partners or was employed in a well-paying job. For the rest of her life, Rosemary would feel compelled to keep working to earn money to sustain them and Barnsley. While to outward appearance she must have seemed like a wealthy woman, she was plagued by money worries for the rest of her life. Earnings from her books, lectures, and garden design commissions provided the means to support herself and her family and keep Barnsley going. Rosemary was then sixty-five.

Once Rosemary turned to it, she was much better at finances than David. She could earn money, which he never really did to sufficient extent. If she had been born a generation later, no doubt she would have finished her studies and gone on to succeed in another arena. Without the constraints and conventions of her class but with her discipline and intelligence, she might well have gone into a profession, such as finance or politics. As Katherine Lambert observed, Rosemary, like Mrs. Thatcher, had "the same mixture of charm and drive and ruthlessness really. I'm sure she would have probably gone completely in another direction, never have set foot in a garden."

But Rosemary was bound by the conventions of her time and class. She had chosen to marry instead of completing her university degree. And even with the few years of independence provided by David's absence during the war, she hadn't chosen to work, even as a volunteer, or create a platform of her own. She was entirely the wife and mother. It would have been out of the ordinary for her to pursue her own career. After David's death, the need to earn money drove her to succeed at a career in horticulture.

Although Rosemary was devastated by David's loss and his absence left her very lonely, over time she did realize that his death freed her from the constraints of their conventional marriage relationship. Even though Rosemary could be very bossy, she was a traditional wife and felt she should defer to David. Her son, Christopher, confirmed that she tried not to outshine David and, although contrary to her nature, tried to play a submissive role. Rosemary acknowledged that she viewed David as "the senior member of the partnership, the umbrella. He was delighted when my first book was published, but he probably thought it was a flash in the pan. Since his death, I have been free to be my own person, to go off anywhere I want."[2]

David's death was a release in the best sense. The decks were cleared and she gathered up all her power. She'd been successful but not nearly as successful as she would become on an international stage. The garden allowed her a socially acceptable platform where she could not only shine, but also earn money through paying visitors, her books, her lectures, and – increasingly – her garden design work for clients. But she was also left alone in that big house without her husband or her children.

Driven both by the financial imperative and her own deep loneliness, she would turn increasingly to her work. And with it, she also turned increasingly to drink. Although few would recall ever seeing Rosemary visibly drunk or out of control, her problem became more pronounced. While her driving was harrowing at best even when sober, she was stopped quite a few times by the police for drunk driving and had her driver's license suspended for a long period of time. Those working for her learned to lie low during the mornings when she appeared especially the worse for wear. And it was her drinking that would invariably cause periodic, serious breaks with friends and relatives.

Being alone, she was happy to have masses of people in the garden all day long and every day, but she plaintively complained that "they all go home at five o'clock and I'm left with no one." "The nights were frightening to her," her friend Tim Rees recalled. More than ever she invited people to come to visit and stay with her. While many of them felt complimented, Rosemary was desperate for company after dark.

America proved the best antidote to her loneliness and her financial worries. It was also where she could shed the trappings of English conventions. During the years David was ill, she had declined any trips to the States but just five months after his death, she returned on her own, traveling to Dallas, New Orleans, Atlanta, and New York. Wherever she went, Americans treated her like royalty, bought her books, and paid her handsomely for her talks and her garden designs. By 1984, she had five books out, all of which were widely available and successful in America. Indeed, over the years, her books would sell far more copies in the United States than in England.[3]

Most importantly, *The American Woman's Garden* gave her a built-in audience in every community where a garden had been featured, and the book included gardens in eighteen states from the grandest to the more modest, from the East Coast to the West, north to south and much in between. The photography was vastly improved in quality since her first book, *The Englishwoman's Garden*.

America was ripe for Rosemary's message that anyone, even a late-blooming, self-taught amateur like herself, could create a beautiful garden. More Americans had become homeowners since the war, when the dream of owning one's own home coupled with suburban growth became a reality. Gardening was an increasingly popular diversion, and with it came a growing sophistication of taste. Although Americans did not have the same tradition of horticulture that was so deeply embedded in British culture, they had greater affluence in the 1980s as the world emerged from the oil crisis of the 1970s.

At first, people paid enormous attention to their lawns and the mandatory foundation plantings around the house. Levittown was the prototype, a planned community of mass produced, affordable homes, each on a separate small plot of land, but linked to the neighbors and the larger community by expansive front lawns. Levittown spawned imitators across the country. In 1980, Ronald Reagan was elected President, and America's economy strengthened. With growing wealth, more ambitious suburban communities developed with grander, custom built homes.

Americans were traveling abroad and developing a taste for things foreign. Julia Child had already popularized French cooking in the 1960s. Americans began to think about gardening as something more than merely maintaining a green lawn and a few foundation plantings with low-maintenance ground covers. Even though there were great gardens in France and Italy, most Americans still looked to England as the quintessential source of inspiration, and Rosemary's message would fall on receptive ears.

In February 1985, Rosemary returned to America for the Philadelphia International Flower Show, the oldest and most prestigious in America. Before going to Philadelphia, she appeared at the newly revived New York Flower Show, the first in that city since earlier efforts ceased in 1971. Its revival, held on a large former steamship pier in Manhattan on the Hudson River, was another indication of the burgeoning horticultural interest. New York resurrected its own Flower Show in order to compete with the famous one in Philadelphia, but it did not survive long.

Philadelphia's show was an annual event that traced its

origins back to 1829. Every year, it had grown in scale and complexity. In 1985, the sponsor, the Pennsylvania Horticultural Society, had chosen as the theme "A Taste of Britain." Rosemary was the star attraction at the gala black-tie dinner on Saturday night, held amidst the fragrance and flowers of the exhibits before the show opened to the public the next day. As usual, the entire American horticultural establishment was present. In addition, every woman who had written an essay for *The American Woman's Garden* was invited, and almost every one of them came.[4]

Holding court at the center table, Rosemary was surrounded by a rapt audience hanging on her every word and taking in each gesture. She behaved like a movie star playing to her fans. As always, she was impeccably dressed, her blue eyes danced and sparkled at every person who greeted her. Invitations flew both ways, and many she encountered resolved to travel to Barnsley. Her American address book, already bursting with names across the country, collected important additions as she scrawled down names and addresses in her inimitable green ink.

Some of the women in the book were quite grand in their own right, with famous names like du Pont and Rockefeller, but each was thrilled to be included. It was a wonderful evening. Like students signing yearbook pages at graduation, the women passed around copies of Rosemary's book to be signed by the others present, each annotating the page featuring their garden.

While in Philadelphia, Rosemary spoke several times during the week-long event and was interviewed on American television. She stayed with her friends, Bill and Nancy Frederick in the Brandywine Valley outside of nearby Wilmington, Delaware, and gave a talk at Longwood Gardens.

Later that year, Bob Dash wrote to her about another

speaking occasion near his own idiosyncratic garden called Madoo in the fashionable beachside community of Sagaponack, in the Hamptons of Long Island. "The Parrish Museum has or will be contacting you to do a lecture with me June 7. I have said yes I would if you would and we would want enormous amounts of money."[5] Their joint talk at the Parrish Art Museum was entitled "Landscape Pleasures: Designers Collaborate with Nature." Bob described it as their "double or dueling spades" and Rosemary's persona was part of the equation. "The dress, the pearls, the encounters, the whatever, but she made it seem that gardening was something you can do. It wasn't arcane . . . just do it. What's the big fuss? She said about pruning, 'It's just like cutting hair.'"

Although Rosemary did little to reveal her sense of insecurity, she confided to her diary that she was quite nervous and felt better after a whiskey. "Otherwise, my knees were wobbling." She found Bob a bit "hard-hitting. He has such wit and vision when he's sober," but he was quite drunk the whole time she was with him. Although she exuded confidence, privately she confessed, "I am hopeless, unprofessional, ignorant, only opinionated. Can't imagine what carries me through."[6] But manage to carry through she certainly did.

Only those closest to her would recognize any lack of self-confidence. She always appeared poised and comfortable in front of an audience, totally charming in any company. Her daughter Veronica who became a psychologist recognized that "one huge driver for her was a degree of insecurity and wanting to prove herself over, over and over again."

After her talk with Bob Dash, there was a very grand dinner party hosted by Fernanda and James Niven (son of the famous actor, David Niven) under a large, beautifully decorated marquee tent. Rosemary was impressed by all the "rich people decked up in jewels. Not as many jewels as in Atlanta, but a fair few." Afterwards, tired, she went back to stay with Bob who "always wants one more drink. Amusing and so do I. So why not." They would become close friends, Bob among the many gay men who were part of her inner circle.

Despite her nervousness, Rosemary clearly loved an audience, and the American audiences loved her. Simon Verity observed that an audience fired her up. She sparkled as the center of their attention, but she was also genuinely interested in people and their lives, not just their gardens. She was also extremely sympathetic about anyone seriously interested in starting a garden, even when they didn't know how. Having experienced that herself, she was very encouraging and empathetic. To some, her British exterior seemed a bit intimidating but that too added to her charm, especially when people discovered her warmth underneath.

Rosemary would travel to the United States virtually every year thereafter, often making several trips per year. At every destination, she would lecture and promote her books. Gregory Long, later President of the New York Botanical Garden, was then working at the New York Public Library where he was responsible for the lecture program. He invited Rosemary to speak and found her very strong and vigorous. He enjoyed her acerbic observations and could tell that it was very important to her to be speaking and that talks would help her to sell her books. After the talk, there was a lunch held for her with the organizing committee and, as she had done with many others she met through her lectures, she invited Gregory to come to Barnsley.

Following her invitation, Gregory did go to Barnsley but he didn't tell Rosemary he was coming. "I saw her in the house and at first, I wasn't going to bother her. . . . She waved at me from the window and came out. She wasn't sure who I was, so she came out and thought this is interesting. We walked around together. We reminded each other of our meeting in New York, then went inside for drinks for a long time. It got dark. It was dinnertime and I needed to be in Bath. She said, 'That's silly. You should stay. We'll have a little supper and you should stay over and drive in the morning.' I didn't do it . . . and I left her there in the dark and she was all alone in that house."

It must have been hard to be back at Barnsley, alone in that big empty house after being feted and fussed over in America. Between trips, she would resume her demanding schedule, managing her own high-maintenance gardens, working on her books and articles, keeping up her growing correspondence, and greeting garden visitors.

With her expanding public life of writing, garden design, and travel, she was lucky to be able to rely on the hard work and continuity of the Bailey brothers who helped to keep Barnsley maintained to perfection. Its reputation grew with hers, attracting ambitious, young gardening talent, eager to come for a stint to enhance their horticultural credentials. That these gardeners would come and go with such little difficulty is largely a credit to the ongoing, steady hands of the Bailey brothers, fixtures there for almost fifteen years.

Rosemary not only used these apprentice gardeners at Barnsley, she also enlisted them to help with her expanding garden design work for clients. For hands-on garden installations, Rosemary often brought her Barnsley gardening team with her to ensure the work was done properly. And from her list of alumni, she often parceled out assignments for them to handle. Eventually, when there were simply too many jobs for her, she generously promoted her coterie to potential clients, suggesting they be hired instead. Thus, without a professional staff but with an expanding network of Barnsley graduates who had once worked for her, she managed to handle a growing garden design business.

Tim Rees, who became a highly regarded garden designer of note, was one at the top of her list. Tim met Rosemary in the early 1980s and became a frequent visitor and weekend guest shortly after David died. Being a handsome young man, he also provided company for Rosemary. "She was like a second grandmother. . . . I used to go down on most weekends. She became a very close friend."

Professionally trained, Tim was a great help when Rosemary was called on for more ambitious work. "She needed to know some of the basics on how to draw plans and present them. That was my part. I could show her about a drawing board and scale. . . . If she had a particularly large job sometimes, she would call me in the initial stage . . . she didn't have that professional training. She was at heart very professional . . . but some of the professional techniques she didn't have. And I think that's where I, amongst others, came in."

Structure had never been Rosemary's strong suit; David had contributed that to Barnsley. "Her medium was in plants. Her perspective was essentially historical. I always remember a visit with Burle Marx." Roberto Burle Marx was the renowned Brazilian landscape designer who created modernist public parks and gardens, using bold sweeps of a single plant and strong structure. Perhaps his most famous design is the pavement at Copacabana Beach in Rio de Janeiro, Brazil. "I have a lovely picture of him with Rosemary wandering around the potager. I remember she took him into her library and took out the ancient books, trying to persuade him that this is where garden design comes from. He had this sort of querulous eyebrow. You couldn't have imagined two more opposite individuals with opposite approaches – probably very similar temperaments at heart. Burle Marx is someone who's essentially his own invention and originality.

Whereas Rosemary I think was always rooted historically in her view of gardens."

Tim Rees helped Rosemary by providing formal drawings of the garden plans she was working on; in turn, Rosemary helped Tim establish his own reputation by recommending him to potential clients. Tim admired her for her generosity, her warm heart, and her courage, but he knew her well enough to appreciate her complexity. He could trust her honesty even when he didn't welcome it. "You would always get the truth. She could be impossible. It was sort of a double-edged sword. Sometimes it came out as bluntness and occasionally if she had a hangover, down right rudeness. I know people who couldn't stand Rosemary Verey, met her at the wrong time."

Tim, like many others, also recalls hair-raising drives with Rosemary. After dinner out with friends, "We both got inebriated. She said, 'It's better that I lose my license rather than you.' We were going on those steep Cotswold banks. We went up the sides of them, then down and round the corners – fantastic!" In commenting on her fearless, courageous qualities, Tim recognized that "she also had a very passionate side to her. From one perspective, she would occupy this particular position in English society of a country lady, of a particular class, with a country house, with her connections and her friendships. And yet also, there was this very adventurous character as well. I think she enjoyed stepping outside that realm and part of that was a major appeal to her of her trips to the States and her friendships in the States. Friendships across a complete range of incomes and class and cultures and she loved it – absolutely adored it – it was a blessed release for her to go over there. And she felt loved."

Sue Spielberg was another gardener who arrived to work alongside Andy and Les Bailey. John Sales, the Gardens

Adviser to the National Trust, was the father of Sue's significant partner, and he suggested Sue contact Rosemary to see if she could apprentice there before applying for formal training at Kew. Rosemary offered the untrained but eager Sue work, saying, "I can't afford very much, but I can pay your petrol money." Sue worked at Barnsley for two years, beginning in 1985, and even though she enjoyed working for Rosemary, knew she "wasn't an easy character to get along with. If she didn't like you or she had an off day, she could be really sharp."

Increasingly, the Barnsley gardens were filled with visitors. What began as a garden open one day a year, and then open one day a week began to open virtually every day as more groups came to see it. As a result of Rosemary's American lecture tours, increasing numbers of Americans arrived eager to see her and the garden. Sue knew that the Americans treated her like royalty, which she loved. And without David, her adoring American audiences filled a hole in her life, along with fees for her talks and proceeds from her books. But success builds on success. As she became ever more popular, she was invited to do more things than she could really handle.

The Bailey brothers were essential to the ongoing management of the garden in her more frequent absences. They learned how to work around Rosemary, and Sue found them "very, very cynical. They were a bit wary sometimes of what mood she would be in and I learned to be wary in the mornings of what mood she would be in as well. Sometimes she'd be as nice as pie, really lovely. And others times she just wouldn't be. Snappy. It depended on what sort of evening she'd had the night before. Or how much she'd had to drink."

Andy and Les were not educated, so there was also a class issue there. If Rosemary enjoyed leaving those issues behind when she went to America, she was highly attuned to status when she returned home. Many others, including Rupert Golby, viewed Rosemary's relationship with the Bailey boys as "quite feudal." Another friend saw them come in to receive their pay from Rosemary, thinking that it was almost as if they were bowing and touching their forelocks before her. Andy and Les were treated as her "garden boys and were always going to be her garden boys." Rosemary continued to tell Andy how to plant potatoes each spring even though he knew perfectly well how to plant them. But Andy and Les could be naughty so long as they were confident they wouldn't be caught. They hazed Sue, sending her out ahead of them to test Rosemary's mood when she came to give them their orders for the day.

One time, Andy instructed Sue to cut down the honesty in early fall, thereby depriving the garden of their beautiful winter translucent papery seed heads. Andy knew Rosemary would be furious and made sure where her anger would be directed. When Sue heard Rosemary calling in her high-pitched voice, "Oooouu – Oooouuu, Sooo-ooo!" she hid behind the summerhouse, pretending not to hear her and hoping Rosemary wouldn't find her, a pattern she repeated on more than one occasion, "But she always did!" Sue is reminded of this experience every time she sees honesty in her own garden.

Despite all the other demands on her time and no matter how talented her team of gardeners, Rosemary refused to completely delegate responsibility for the gardens. Her eye and her decisions kept the gardeners on their toes. She continually introduced new plants, ruthlessly removed those past their prime and ensured that nothing grew tired or stale. But after issuing the day's commands, she would leave it to the gardeners and withdraw indoors to her desk. Working in the morning room, she could look out over the garden. Sue thought, "It just epitomized the very English country-house style. She had this oval table where she'd do her work with a beautiful floral tablecloth hanging down. Lovely antiques everywhere and books and that smell. She'd have fresh flowers in the house and go out and get a little posy of hellebores and have them floating in a big wide shallow dish and piles of books everywhere. You couldn't really sit down anywhere because there'd be things she'd have to deal with and pile of the things that she'd have to read and piles of books that were reference books for her writing. It felt warm because she kept a log fire burning in there most of the time and it just had that smell and that look."

The gardeners knew they had to follow "Rosemary's Rules." A favorite was "Time and Motion" repeated and repeated until it became ingrained. Rosemary would demonstrate how to perform a task efficiently without wasting time. Ever the teacher, Rosemary expected her staff to follow instructions. One lesson of Time and Motion took place in her potting shed where the staff was to pot up rooted cuttings. First, she demonstrated how everything required was to be placed readily at hand. This assembly-line approach streamlined the repetitive task and increased efficiency.

Another of Rosemary's Rules was to stand up straight. While using long-handled clippers to edge the borders, one gardener received a surprisingly sharp poke in the back, as Rosemary reprimanded, "There are miles of edges in this border which you will never finish if you don't stand up straight!"[7]

Just as she drew upon superb gardening talent, Rosemary was astute to encourage photographers to come to Barnsley. She became close friends with two of the most brilliant,

Jerry Harpur and Andrew Lawson. Their magnificent photographs adorned her new books and helped promote Barnsley as a must-see garden stop.

Jerry Harpur first met Rosemary just before David died and as he was beginning his career in garden photography. At the time, there were almost no photographers specializing in gardens. Rosemary was eager to have him photograph Barnsley. "She was nothing, if not ambitious, of course." She invited Jerry Harpur to come and stay with her for two weeks so he could make a record of what her garden actually looked like. She was "very keen for that, and she was keen to go down in history as one of the great women gardeners like Vita Sackville-West." Having other demands on his time, as well as living quite a distance away in Essex, Jerry could not accept Rosemary's invitation, but he remained an important photographer of Barnsley as well as a devoted friend for the rest of Rosemary's life.

Soon after Jerry, Andrew Lawson arrived. He lived closer by in Oxfordshire and was able to come to Barnsley often. He, too, was just making his way as a garden photographer when he came to photograph Barnsley, composing his photographs almost like the paintings he created when he wasn't photographing. As a result of "encouraging people like me and Jerry and other people like us, this garden did get a huge amount of publicity. She was very clever at encouraging photographers. Not many garden owners do that. A lot of people resent photographers and find them intrusive, which they are really. Sort of stomping around the place, taking pictures." Barnsley was extremely photogenic. Andrew "thought of Rosemary's garden as being a collection of theater sets."

One of Andrew's marvelous and early photographs was of the laburnum walk in its full glory with the beautiful purple allium in bloom underneath. "It is the under planting that made it and it was also the sundial at the end. It made the focal point for it. It's very intimate, but in the pictures, it looks pretty huge and grand." Having seen Andrew's stunning, almost monumental, image of the Laburnum Walk, visitors were often slightly disappointed when they arrived at Barnsley to discover how small it actually was. "We use wide angle lenses that make things look bigger and people always come, having seen the pictures thinking it's going to be much bigger."

When Andrew arrived to take his photograph, "the laburnum was absolutely perfect. I was really excited. And I thought how Rosemary would like this to be perfect. I'm going to make it even more perfect than this. I'm going to sweep up the little flowers that have fallen off the laburnum. So I hunted around and I found the tool shed and I found a broom and I swept the whole thing clean. And I got my photograph absolutely pristine. And I said (to Rosemary), 'The laburnum looks absolutely perfect and I made it even more perfect by sweeping up.' 'Oh no! I love the flowers on the ground,' she said. 'It's like a carpet.' And I said 'Well don't bother because by lunchtime they will be back.' And we were friends for life after that."

Jerry thought that Rosemary "had immense style. Style is a very good word to apply to Rosemary and that informed the way that she did her garden. The laburnum with the alliums that we photographed is I think the most famous view of any garden anywhere in the world."

In 1987, *The New Englishwoman's Garden* came out, Rosemary's first book to appear since David's death three years before. Virtually all the photographs were taken by Jerry Harpur and Andrew Lawson. The format was again based on *The Englishwoman's Garden*, and there must have been some truce declared, because it was co-edited with

Alvilde Lees-Milne. This time Alvilde wrote an essay on her own new garden at Essex House, at Badminton. The foreword was written by Hardy Amies, Rosemary's friend and clothing designer for the Queen.

There would be another book (and in one year two books) each year thereafter for the next decade. Towards the end of the 1980s, with her horticultural star ascendant, Rosemary was about to face two momentous developments in her life, each involving a man named Charles. The first happy development involved H.R.H. The Prince of Wales; the second, and more challenging, involved her oldest son.

CHAPTER EIGHT

Leaving Barnsley House;
Prince Charles Arrives
Late 1980s

And now, he's absolutely one of my best friends.

OUR YEARS AFTER David's death, as she was about to turn seventy, Rosemary decided to give Barnsley House to her oldest son, Charles. She moved into The Close, following the pattern set by David's parents when they gave Barnsley House to David, and then moved into the renovated adjacent stable-cum-garage and called it The Close. Unlike Cecil and Linda Verey, who had only one son, Rosemary had four children, so it is hard to fully understand this decision. Some of her closest friends tried cautioning her against it; one of them advised her to take proper financial advice before giving away the house.[1]

It may well be that her decision was indeed partly the result of professional advice; taxes probably had something to do with it. Under the applicable English gift and estate tax rules, if someone made a gift and lived at least seven years thereafter, there would be no gift or estate tax on the transferred property. One would have expected the solicitors handling David's estate to raise this tax strategy. But one has to wonder why Rosemary didn't give Barnsley House to all her children, or at least to a trust for their benefit. Why did she choose to give it solely to Charles?

David's will did not favor Charles above his other children. To the contrary, he provided for all four of them equally. His will did not require or request Rosemary to give the house to Charles, nor did it give the house to Charles in the event Rosemary failed to survive David.[2] In his will of April 29, 1984, signed just days before he died, he bequeathed Barnsley House and its gardens to Rosemary but oddly he excluded The Close and his other land holdings; he also excluded his interest in the Arlington Mill partnership, which he held with his daughters, Veronica and Davina. The will also left Rosemary all of his personal belongings but, in a rather old-fashioned way, left all the rest of his estate in a trust for Rosemary's benefit for her life, rather than giving her outright ownership. On her death, the will directed the trust to end and pass to all four children in equal shares (or to their issue if any one of them was not then living).[3] David named Rosemary and his lawyer, John Humphrey Colquhoun, to be his executors and trustees.

Even though David appeared not to favor Charles above his other children, Rosemary's daughter Veronica believes that by giving Barnsley to Charles, Rosemary felt she was carrying out David's wishes. Whether carrying out David's wishes or not, she was following a well-established British tradition of primogeniture, a custom still prevalent in certain British circles to favor the oldest son with the lion's share of the family's fortune. To modern observers, it seems positively Dickensian to leave the family estate to the oldest son, with the younger sons forced to earn their own way in the army or the church and the daughters expected to marry well to restore the family coffers. In many ways, Rosemary was a conventional English lady and Charles was the oldest son. She gave him the house and moved into the Dower, conforming to upper-class tradition and what she must have felt was expected of her.

It did not prove to be a happy arrangement for either of them. Understandably, once he owned the house, Charles felt he was in charge and tried to assert his authority but Rosemary was not willing to let go. She certainly did not defer to him. Barnsley was her stage and she was still the star, running the garden and welcoming ever-increasing numbers of visitors virtually every day. Even when the garden was officially closed, she would often relent, allowing eager visitors to come in anyway.

Charles was then forty-seven years old; he, with his wife, Denzil, and their daughter, Amy, took up residence in the main house. But the house overlooked and opened out to Rosemary's gardens, and it must have been difficult for his family to cope with all those visitors. Her sister-in-law, Gill thought, "It was too near. And Rosemary didn't know about standing back. It was a barking mad idea!"

In her later years, when looking back in a rare contemplative moment, Rosemary wondered aloud whether she might have been better off moving to some small property with a lovely view, removing herself entirely from this strained arrangement. She rarely revealed her inner feelings to others but she did say, "I should have just gone!"[4] Others agreed, but understood why she couldn't really move out. "It was her theater. The magic went on really because she was still there."[5]

The strain between Rosemary and Charles was palpable, and visitors could sense it. "You could tell that Charles was doing his best, but his best was clearly not enough for his mother."[6] With the high standards she set for herself and all who were part of her life, it was almost impossible to do enough to please her. "You could feel the tension."[7] Far worse for their relationship was the ongoing challenge of Charles's personal financial difficulties. He did try. He produced and sold heavy teak garden furniture, benches, chairs and tables, which Rosemary helped promote. Denzil began to sell antiques from a space inside the main house that opened into the garden. But, like his father, Charles was not good about financial matters, and unlike his father, he didn't have other assets to use to settle his debts. If the bank decided to foreclose on Charles, it could only look to Barnsley House. That threatened Rosemary. She had to continue to bail him out.

Nevertheless, Rosemary had made her decision and was determined to live with it. Before moving into The Close, she arranged for renovations to suite her taste and sense of style. She added a large glass conservatory and called upon her friend, Simon Verity, to work his magic inside. She then went off for a couple of months on a lecture tour to Australia, leaving Simon in charge.

Accompanied by Jerry Harpur, Rosemary made the long trip to Australia where the ABC Melbourne affiliate would sponsor her talk at the Melbourne Art Gallery. They had booked her into a room that could hold one hundred people; to their surprise they sold so many tickets they had to move the talk to a much larger hall seating seven hundred. Interestingly, she was not "massively well received." Perhaps as a Commonwealth country and unlike America, the Australians didn't take well to her British accent; Jerry thought the audience felt "she was talking down to them." Since Rosemary never talked down to her audience, it seems more likely that the Australians were reacting to her very British upperclass style.

While Rosemary was away, work on The Close progressed rapidly. Simon had been given carte blanche, but she had requested him to create a grotto in her new conservatory. Simon installed his grotto on the interior wall. Water dripped over rough stones imbedded with shells, falling into a small pool. The conservatory would become a cheerful living space, filled with light and the sound of falling water, the air scented by fragrant plants. He also added sparkle to what became Rosemary's formal library-living room, an otherwise dark interior room that would rarely be used other than to store her library and occasionally entertain visitors. Simon's frieze along the ceiling was a masterpiece sculpted out of plaster enhanced with bits of mirror and precious lapis lazuli; it reflected any light that managed to pierce the gloom. Rosemary loved it. She said, "It's like daylight coming through."[8]

There was also a handsome dining room with French doors opening out onto a small private terrace overlooking one end of the garden. The dining room served as Rosemary's work space; the table was almost always covered with books, projects, slides, and correspondence, all piled in an order known only to her. At the far end of the room, a desk and typewriter sat at the ready.

The nearby kitchen was an informal, functional affair, warmed by her Aga stove. The Aga is a peculiar creation, popular in unheated or under-heated English country houses. It is almost like placing a furnace in the kitchen. Fueled by oil, the Aga is always on, ready to cook anything, anytime. Besides its cooking function, it warms the room, serving as the perfect place to drape wet clothes to dry or to restore cold hands. The gardening staff customarily took their "elevenses," or coffee break, huddled around the Aga.

Rosemary ate most of her meals in the kitchen, often with guests, at the oilcloth-draped table in the center, because it was often too cold to eat in the conservatory. Only on rare occasions, such as Christmas or Boxing Day, did Rosemary clear the dining room table for a formal dinner there, removing the countless piles of books and papers. Upstairs, Rosemary's bedroom was adorned with a wall covered in botanical prints. Nearby, her bathroom with lovely tiles adjoined another bath that served a second small bedroom down the hall for her frequent guests. She moved in to The Close in March of 1988, the same year she received the prestigious Christie's Historic Houses Association's Garden of the Year Award.

Despite this major upheaval, she continued to be productive, to write, manage the garden, welcome visitors, and travel to America as well as to Europe. Following a long hiatus after David's death, her books resumed their regular appearance; *The New Englishwoman's Garden* came out the year before the move. She also began work on what many regard as her most significant book, *The Garden in Winter*. Her garden design work continued to expand as well, and this with her heavy overseas travel schedule forced her to give up writing her regular column for *Country Life*.

Katherine Lambert appeared on the scene to help with *The Garden in Winter*. A highly educated woman who lived nearby, she would thereafter become a significant partner in Rosemary's writings and life, serving as her personal assistant, secretary, and editor. When she first arrived, Rosemary presented her with a challenge, perhaps a test. She pointed to a huge array of boxes full of her slides and asked Katherine to take a look and "sort things out." It was an impossible task. The slides were in a complete jumble, including everything in Rosemary's life going back to her childhood. Katherine's spirits sank in despair, until Rosemary, charming as she could be, made it all seem not only possible but fun.

In the end, Katherine persuaded her to jettison the idea of using her slides as the basis of the book and instead treat them as an *aide-mémoire*. "Rosemary then approached the book from the cerebral, the literary, the words, rather than from the pictures. I was feeling completely exhausted having pilloried all these millions of slides, but she said 'Let's have a glass of champagne to seal the bargain.' " So Katherine began to work for her on far more than just books. "You know what Rosemary was like. [I] ended up doing everything, really, from making the flowers to cleaning the loos . . . as well as helping her with articles, books and letters and everything else in between."

Katherine admired Rosemary's formidable energies and ability to work on many fronts simultaneously. "I think . . . multi-tasking was invented specifically for Rosemary. She had the most phenomenal ability to compartmentalize. . . . She'd be working very hard on a chapter of a book and then she'd look at her watch and sort of mid-flow say 'Oh, I've got five minutes before I've got to meet someone.' She was absolutely able to switch off. And then it's on to the next thing that she gave an equal amount of attention to and then at three o'clock in the morning she'd get up to work on one of her books. So this ability to focus . . . an awful lot of it I think had to do with her mathematical mind."

At one point, Katherine and Rosemary had a serious falling out, a pattern she would repeat with others, especially when she had been drinking. "I think it was the first time that her son, Christopher, realized she had a drinking problem. I arrived and for some reason Rosemary was definitely the worse for wear. She absolutely flew at me and attacked me because I hadn't parked my car in exactly the place that she thought I should. Or something really so stupid and so I just thought, I've had it, so I just left." Katherine stayed away for almost a year until Rosemary reached out to call her back. "She was a very difficult employer for all her staff. It's like being around a fascinating snake, rather beautiful and fascinating, but you also knew it had a venom in it – and it could pounce on you, without warning." She was "very empowering, but she was also fairly crushing. A strange combination. A woman of great contradictions all around."

These storms were more likely to be directed against women than men, toward people who worked for her rather than those who were important to her.[9] But she could be difficult even to men, especially if they worked for or with her. Her friend, Tim Rees, felt that most of the time she was "a wonderful, engaging passionate human being with a lovely chuckle when something amused her, [but] she could strike the fear of God into you if you caught her when she was busy, dealing with a deadline or a hangover. You learnt to approach Rosemary at the right time and in the right place – and sometimes to beat a hasty retreat."

The Garden in Winter proved much more than another beautiful picture book; it was a serious piece of writing with a significant lesson addressing a then-ignored topic. At first, Rosemary expected to produce this book along the format of her earlier works, relying on essays written by others and pulling them together without having to write very much herself. She asked the Duchess of Devonshire and Beth Chatto, among others, to contribute essays, but each politely turned her down. So Rosemary wrote the entire book herself.

Erica Hunningher, at the time the editorial director of the publisher Frances Lincoln, arrived to work with her on the book. Erica first visited Rosemary while she was still living at the big house before she moved into The Close and recalls an initial spat they had over the pronunciation of plant names. Erica said "*Clematis tangutica,*" emphasizing the last two syllables as "*tee*-ka." This prompted Rosemary's retort. "Erica, plant names are not all pronounced as if they were Italian! The emphasis isn't always on the penultimate syllable, and it's pronounced Tang-*oooo*-tica." Erica replied "Thank you Rosemary. I want to be corrected, but I will learn better if you told me nicely. I don't want to be ticked off." Or to cry. They got on brilliantly after that.

The Garden in Winter's message was that a garden could and should look wonderful in all the seasons of the year. Always the teacher, she opens the book with "A Plea for the Garden in Winter," speaking directly to the reader. "A garden in winter is the absolute test of the true gardener. Fair-weather gardeners are to gardens what interior decorators are to buildings – they know only half the story. If your garden looks good in winter, you belong to a select band capable of bending nature to its will. If you master the worst that winter can throw at you – ice, snow, wind without remorse – you will have a sense of conquest."[10]

Barnsley serves as the laboratory, making the case through the brilliant photographs of Andrew Lawson that show off the strong structures in the low winter light, the green box balls and the knot garden touched by a dusting of frost. Here Rosemary's plantsmanship is on display, with a focus on foliage, texture, berries, and branches. The shapes and structure are clearly visible in the spare winter landscape, after all the color of the flowers has passed and the deciduous trees have dropped their leaves.

The book is divided into four main sections, with sub-chapters within: Space, Structure & Pattern; Winter Pictures; Winter Colour; and Work & Pleasure. Detailed Plant Portraits are at the back of the book. Rosemary's character is evident when she says, "Many years ago I learned that if you wake up on a winter morning with the rain beating against your window, although you may feel there is little incentive to go outside, the reality is quite different. . . . Somehow the wind is never so fierce nor the rain so unpleasant as you imagined. . . . When you get back home, your cheeks will be glowing and your approach to the day positive."[11]

Rosemary didn't forget her American readers, well aware that her books had a bigger market in the United States than England. Unlike other English garden writers, she paid attention to the plant and climate differences. She wrote, "I am well aware than in many American states, winter is much longer and much colder than ours – the snow deeper, the moment of thaw more dramatic and the onset of spring swifter. I appreciate that my task of nursing my garden through winter is much easier than that of my gardening friends in the Midwest – I am glad to be in England. But then if God had standardized the weather, half the joy of gardening would be lost."[12]

The topic was revolutionary to many who assumed that they and their gardens could simply hibernate during the winter months. Rosemary's message awoke her audience to the idea of planting for winter interest, an idea that has since become obvious. But at the time it was novel and the book had tremendous impact. Her writing was clear and understandable, "very like a personal letter, very practical. She got very much to the point and she was very good about just telling you about plants that she really liked. You could see the enthusiasm."[13] One American reviewer, Allen Lacy, called *The Garden in Winter* a "lyrical text."[14]

Many of Rosemary's gardening clients and friends believe they had a role in suggesting this topic to Rosemary. One close American friend from Dallas, Carl Neels, himself a creative garden designer, believes he suggested this topic to Rosemary because the summer months are so punishing in Texas that Carl viewed the cooler months of winter as a better time to garden. Hilary Weston believes her own garden in Canada inspired Rosemary to write the book. "She looked out the window and saw hoar frost on all the branches of the bare trees, the light was shining through them. And

Rosemary said, they are just like ice sculptures." However the idea arose, Rosemary made it her own. Her book *The Garden in Winter* is a classic.

Just as Rosemary was about to move into The Close, another brilliant gardener, Rupert Golby arrived to work for her. Rupert, fully trained at Kew, had been the head gardener on a large estate when his employer fell on hard times. Lord Say and Sele, who lived at nearby Broughton Castle and was a long time close friend of the Vereys, heard he was out of work and offered to take him to meet Rosemary, hoping she might be able to find him a new position. Instead, she offered him a job at Barnsley. But there was a problem; Rosemary was used to being head gardener, and she wasn't used to having people work for her after studying at Kew, especially someone who had been in charge of running a garden. Rupert had a hard time settling in, but they worked out a truce of sorts and he stayed on.

Rupert went on to develop his own fame and fortune as a gifted garden designer and much of his success was due to Rosemary's support.[15] When inundated with work she couldn't possibly cope with, she passed much of it on to Rupert. In the final phase of his six-month stint for her, "she was suddenly very warm towards me and we got on famously and then after I left she became hugely supportive and gave me countless jobs."

To this day, Rupert credits Rosemary with helping train his eye and raise his standards. "Nobody cleans a garden like she would clean the garden." He especially recalled the daily dead heading. He began to dead head the delphinium, then at full height with some dead blooms at the bottom of a few stalks. "She said to me, 'You must . . . cut those dead flowers off the delphiniums and so I did. I cut them [the stalks] off at the bottom. And she came out kind of half way through, saw me and sort of screamed and said 'What are you doing?!' She said not like that, she just meant the florets, the individual florets, not the stalks, and she then waded in to the border with me and looked at what I had done, snatched my secateurs and showed me how to do it and then walked back and got my secateurs and flung them across the lawn and marched off. I didn't see her again that day." But that searing experience "helped me in all my gardens, to give me that standard . . . and a critical eye."

From Rosemary, Rupert learned how to use plants like building blocks, to use a large group of the same plant in order to make a big impact. She was constantly re-evaluating and editing as plants matured, ruthlessly cutting down any tree or shrub that had grown out of scale to the composition. And she would edit and revise plantings with new thoughts and ideas, never allowing her garden to grow stale or static. Rupert watched Rosemary work in the garden hands on. "She was quite smart, came from quite a good family, but she didn't mind getting out there and grubbing about with her hands. Great big rings all covered in compost. She hated anybody who stood back when there was hard work to be done because she would pitch in and get the broom out, get the bucket out, clean things up."

As Rosemary was in the process of moving into The Close, something wondrous occurred to soothe her soul. H.R.H. The Prince of Wales arrived on the scene. Rosemary was having breakfast with some visiting Americans when the phone rang. One of the Americans said, "Rosemary, take it. It could be the most important phone call of your life." Rosemary then picked up the phone and heard a voice saying, "This is the Prince of Wales." In reply, and sure that her American friends were pulling her leg, Rosemary said, "Oh come on, it's much too early in the morning for jokes! Come on. Who is this?!"[16] However, Rosemary's recollection of this first telephone conversation was somewhat more nuanced. She said, "I always imagine I said, 'You must be joking,' but I don't know whether I did or not."[17]

Indeed it was Prince Charles and he wasn't joking. He asked, "What are you doing today?" In reply, she said "Well, I hope Sir that maybe I'm going to see you. Would you like to come over?" And that's exactly what he did. His own property, called Highgrove, was just outside the village of Tetbury, only a short drive away from Barnsley. He arrived to walk through the garden and sit in the potager to talk. The "next thing that happened was he said would I come to help him with a bit of the garden which we call the Cottage Garden which is fairly close to the house at Highgrove. And ever since then, he's absolutely one of my best friends."

It was a stroke of good fortune that Highgrove happened to be so near Barnsley. In his thank you note to her, Prince Charles apologizes for his "dreadful short notice" and modestly imagines "it must have been somewhat annoying for you to have yet more visitors. No doubt you wanted to have a quiet and untroubled day. But to have had visitors who stayed so long was little short of insufferable and I do apologize if we prevented you from doing anything else."[18] He thanked her for her generous gifts of plants from her garden center, all of which had been promptly planted, a leather hat box, "which has an eminent position on the table in the hall and looks very distinguished. The books you gave me are treasured mementos of Barnsley and of my new-found gardening friend and I am enormously grateful." He then invited her to come to look at "my astonishingly unprofessional garden."

That visit began a warm and particularly happy relationship that continued for the rest of Rosemary's life; it was a friendship that she would treasure. Prince Charles was then not quite forty years old and Rosemary almost seventy. The fact that the Prince of Wales asked Rosemary to design a part of Highgrove's gardens only added luster to her growing reputation, particularly in England where royalty matters.

Prince Charles was no passive partner, but very much an active participant in the ideas, decisions, and plantings of his gardens. He invited Rosemary to come to Highgrove and welcomed her advice. Rosemary described him as "full of ideas, he's very outgoing, he's very grateful for what you do. . . . And I've worked there with him. Not for him but with him. We've dug together and I've dug with the princes. Lovely little William when he was much smaller."[19]

Prince Charles had acquired Highgrove in the early 1980s when it was just a flat piece of ground surrounding a handsome manor house and began to develop a garden there. He first sought advice from Dame Miriam Rothschild, an early conservationist particularly interested in butterflies and wildflowers, about establishing wildflower meadows. Later he consulted Lady Salisbury, who had restored and created her own impressive gardens at Hatfield House, once home to young Queen Elizabeth I.

Lady Salisbury established the formal garden areas around the house at Highgrove, as well as the outlines of the woodland. She also designed the Walled Garden in a handsome large square space that reflected Rosemary's own style of patterned beds, flowering plants, and careful succession of vegetables and fruits. If Lady Salisbury had not already designed the Walled Garden, Rosemary might have been asked to work on it herself. A perfect assignment, given her own much-admired Potager. But the Walled Garden was already planted when Rosemary arrived on the scene.

Rosemary first worked on an informal border she called

ABOVE: *The frog fountain by Simon Verity.*

LEFT: *Simon Verity's statue of the hunting lady.*

ABOVE: *Holdenby House, Northampton.*

BELOW: *The Little House, in Barnsley Village.*

ABOVE: *Fort Belvedere, Windsor Great Park, Surrey.*

BELOW: *Rosemary Verey's model garden at the Chelsea Flower Show, 1992.*

LEFT: *Rosemary Verey in her conservatory after moving into The Close.*

BELOW: *Tools hung in the potting shed at Barnsley House, each tool kept in its proper place by the painted outline.*

BOTTOM: *Rosemary Verey with her friends and favorite photographers, Andrew Lawson (left) and Jerry Harpur.*

the Cottage Garden. It was in a rather awkward, long, and somewhat narrow area, with hedges along one side leading away from the more formal areas near the house out toward more informal areas in the direction of a newly developing woodland. Prince Charles wanted a new garden there and outlined the general layout of the borders. Lady Salisbury thought it a rather difficult place, an area that could just as well have been left alone in a more natural state with a simple mown path running through it. But she felt that Rosemary made something good out of it, with excellent plantings that continue to exist as she intended.

To suit the challenging site, Rosemary selected the plants for the long informal curving border that she filled with cottage-type flowering plants as well as some trees and shrubs for structure. This was not Rosemary's preferred style; she would have been far more at home in the more formal areas at Highgrove. Her own parterres with their clearly delineated outlines or her knot garden with its intricate shapes, or her potager with its geometry, box edging and box balls, would almost always be her approach when she designed gardens for others. The Cottage Garden at Highgrove was another matter entirely.

Because Prince Charles, Princess Diana, and their two young sons usually spent the summers in Scotland, Rosemary planned the Cottage Garden for spring interest, with later fall color. Unlike her husband, Princess Diana had no interest in the garden or Rosemary's work. "It's no good having a huge array of plants flowering when he's in Scotland which is the end of August and September. He's there at Highgrove in the springtime. So we've planted drifts of Narcissus, Daffodils, and in his meadow, we've planted a large number of Camassias. They are blue flowers that come up through the grass and flower at the same time as some deep red tulips."[20]

Given the general curving outline, Rosemary concentrated on the choice of plants and their combinations, focusing on the mix of colors and the timing and coordination of blooms. Although she often praised her reliance on "squared paper" as essential to her plans, she was far more comfortable having the plants on hand and to point out where they were to go, modifying her paper plans on the spot. She described the process herself, writing, "First, I make a general plan, showing paths, border shapes, prominent features, including any major tree-planting." But then, "I simply make lists of plants for each area, because I really like to lay the plants out on the site."[21]

Rosemary enjoyed working directly with the gardeners. Prince Charles asked her to help select a head gardener for Highgrove so she participated in the choice of David Magson, who came to Highgrove in 1989 and stayed through the late 1990s. Having helped to select him, Rosemary took Magson under her wing, worked well with him and helped him along. She also recommended James Aldridge, who had worked briefly at Barnsley and understood Rosemary's standards; James had learned a huge amount working at Barnsley, finding it a "wonderful environment to work in. With specific attention to detail, management, basic hands on." James came to work with David Magson and together they implemented Rosemary's plans for the Cottage Garden. And, as usual, Rosemary brought in her home team of the Bailey brothers, who worked many hours there. John Hill was also called upon to provide some of the larger plants.

Once the Cottage Garden was underway, Rosemary began to design a shrub border for the area just beyond. Again, a plan involving groups of shrubs rather than herbaceous borders was not her usual style. David Magson, James Aldridge, and Rosemary spent many hours at her kitchen table in The

Close after dinner, pouring through catalogues of plants. David enjoyed her enthusiasm and, although much younger, marveled as she worked long hours into the night, wishing he had half her energy.[22]

Rosemary also introduced Sir Roy Strong to Prince Charles. Sir Roy had earned his own prominence and recognition both as author and as head of the Victoria and Albert Museum in London. He and his wife, Julia, an accomplished stage designer, had become good friends of Rosemary's. They were developing their own gardens at The Laskett in Herefordshire. The hedges had already been planted at Highgrove, but Prince Charles thought he would like to have some "windows" cut through the hedges. Rosemary said, "Roy Strong is good at topiary – he ought to do this." So Sir Roy came and "designed and cut the topiary in the hedges. She brought me in. Very kind of her." He recalls that Rosemary and Prince Charles had "a very tender relationship. . . . She was thrilled. It was her favorite thing. . . . I remember her talking about planting bulbs with him . . . and she was there actually planting and he came out on a weekend and the two of them planted bulbs."

Rosemary also advised on the choice of plants for Prince Charles' developing woodland, although once again she was unable to draw on her own experience because there was no true woodland at Barnsley where even the Wilderness was hardly a woodland. However, Rosemary loved any occasion to be at Highgrove, any excuse to spend time with Prince Charles. She experimented with shade-loving plants in the informality of his woodland, but it did not draw upon her own taste or expertise.

Not surprisingly, there is virtually nothing left of her work in the woodland. It has been replaced by bold designs created by the currently popular garden designers, Julian and

Isabel Bannerman, who later assumed important roles at Highgrove. The Woodland now includes their Stumpery. Once a Victorian garden oddity, a stumpery uses upended tree roots to support ferns, hellebores, and other shade-lovers. At Highgrove, the huge, upended trees lie on their sides, their grotesque masses of roots waving in the air in a way never intended for tree roots. Rosemary probably would have hated it.

Because Rosemary ruled her gardeners with an iron rod, they in turn could rebel. As Highgrove continued to expand and develop and the Prince spent more of his time there, it was opened to the public year round. Prince Charles asked David Magson to modify Rosemary's design for longer seasonal interest; he also wanted bolder colors "to make it a bit more vibrant." Rosemary's preferred palette favored pastels, primarily soft pinks, purples, and lavenders. David Magson and James Aldridge went ahead without her. Perhaps because one of them had worked for Rosemary at Barnsley, he probably took some perverse pleasure in this, since Rosemary could be, and often was, hard on her own help. "The Prince instructed us to do it, so we did a planting plan, and we didn't include Rosemary, which was a bit naughty, really," David recalled.[23]

Both David and James knew she could be ferocious when crossed and would be enraged at their making changes without consulting her. They were right. When Rosemary found out, she was in a fury. She wrote a tough letter berating them for pre-empting her role in re-working the Cottage Garden. She appropriated their plans and "re-jigged them." When the final plan emerged to be presented to the Prince, it was titled "From David, James and Rosemary" but went on to say "Drawn by Rosemary."

Her work at Highgrove and her friendship with Prince

Charles gave Rosemary her greatest pleasure. She delighted in bringing special friends to Highgrove and loved the cachet of being able to open the doors there. After they became friends, she arranged for Oscar de la Renta, the famous fashion designer, to arrive by helicopter for a tour. She brought Christopher Lloyd. Occasionally she would introduce her friends to Prince Charles if he happened to be there. Gregory Long, President of the New York Botanical Garden, went to have tea with Rosemary and Prince Charles. "She was just like a nice English lady meeting with Prince Charles. She wasn't flirtatious with him . . . in the way she was with all those American men who liked her. She was pretty formal and pretty old fashioned and sweet . . . just herself. Not a celebrity. She didn't flash her celebrity status with him. And he was the same with her. Very sweet."

She arranged to have David Wheeler, the founding editor of the literary quarterly garden journal, *Hortus*, come to interview Prince Charles for a book he was writing. David Wheeler first met her while she was still living in the big house as he was starting *Hortus*. She loved *Hortus* and was among its first and strongest promoters. When they arrived, the Prince was recovering from a polo accident with his arm in a sling. David recalls Rosemary said something like, "Sir, you're so wonderful about all this, you behaved so marvelously and you must be in such pain." The Prince replied, "But Rosemary, you don't understand, a thousand years of breeding has gone into this." Unlike Gregory Long, David Wheeler thought Rosemary did indeed flirt with the Prince. "My goodness, she could flirt with him beautifully."

Her writer friend, Stephen Lacey, remembers attending some garden event in Bristol where he had gone with Rosemary to watch the Prince of Wales open it. Instead of heading back to London as planned, Stephen Lacey succumbed to Rosemary's insistence that he come and spend the night at Barnsley, promising they would stop at Highgrove on the way home. "We just turned up at Highgrove and we were wandering around in the vegetable garden and I happened to glance up and see the royal standard being raised on top of the house . . . and then I stepped out from behind this fruit tree, and there was the Prince of Wales who absolutely jumped out of his skin. He was clearly not expecting a stranger in the middle of his vegetable garden. That was fun."

Despite the success of her book *The Garden in Winter* and her work for Prince Charles, Rosemary always felt pressed for money so she was persuaded by her neighbor and friend, Anne Norman, to offer a horticultural school at Barnsley. Seeing how generous Rosemary was with her expertise and time, always ready to offer advice to the many visitors who came to Barnsley and to her readers through her writings, Anne thought a school would be a good way for Rosemary to pass on her knowledge and ensure an income. It proved an enormous amount of work on top of Rosemary's already full plate.

Rosemary responsibly put together a simple business plan, projecting eleven subscribers at £395 each, with a few cheaper slots available for students. After paying for the speakers, lunches, and printing costs, if the total income came to £5,083, Rosemary hoped to net £510. Anne felt while it wasn't a lot, it was quite good money for those days. There were two sessions of one class per week for eight weeks, one in the summer months of May and June and the other an autumn session in October and November.[24]

Attractive flyers with a picture of Barnsley on the cover were printed, offering "Gardening at Barnsley House, Courses for 1988" with eight weekly sessions on Tuesdays. The program started at 10 A.M. with coffee served, then a lecture, a coffee break, the second lecture, followed by lunch and practical work outdoors in the garden all afternoon. Prominent lecturers included Penelope Hobhouse and Rosemary's own coterie of John Hill, Rupert Golby (who arrived to work at Barnsley that March), Tim Rees, and – on a few occasions – Rosemary herself. Because Rosemary was living in The Close, there wasn't a lot of room to hold the fifteen or so people for both the indoor lectures and lunch. That meant they had to clear out the dining room before each Tuesday class. Rosemary "would hate it when we would clear her table that morning. Put the cloth on in order to give everyone lunch and wine. Put everything back after."

Whenever there was a cancellation, Rosemary graciously called to invite her neighbor, Jane Wykeham-Musgrave, to come for free. Jane thought the lectures were particularly good and remembers when both Penelope Hobhouse, by then an equally renowned younger garden-writer designer herself, and Rosemary spoke one day. Afterwards, Jane, who like Rosemary had been a fine horsewoman, bought one of Rosemary's books, which Rosemary signed, saying, "After horses comes gardening." "Hear, hear," wrote Penelope, signing underneath.

This school at Barnsley was very well received by those lucky enough to attend, but Rosemary never repeated the classes again. She was far too busy with other more profitable work. At the start of the next decade, Rosemary would be involved with well-paid work for royalty of another sort. The popular music star Elton John would enter her orbit.

CHAPTER NINE

Elton John, The King of Rock
Early 1990s

He is a perfectionist, which is really good.

OSEMARY VEREY AND Elton John sound like a study in contrasts – he, the King of Rock, she, the Queen of Horticulture, each stars in their own orbit. Together they must have been quite a pair. In dress and appearance, Rosemary was the quintessential English country lady, with her white hair, pearls, spectacles, and flowery dresses. Elton John favored flamboyance. Somehow the two opposites attracted. Perhaps they recognized the same shared qualities of drive and love of audience in each other. When they came together, Rosemary was in her seventies, and Elton John was in his forties.

Elton John was just beginning to develop the gardens at his Berkshire estate called Woodside, located on the outskirts of London near Windsor. It was destined to be as dramatic a production as its show-biz owner. A project that occupied a large cadre of professionals over many years, it was a tribute to Rosemary that Elton John felt he had to enlist her on his garden team. He could certainly pay for and command the attention of anyone he chose, and he demanded the best. Woodside had a vast budget, at one point said to be £96,000 a year. This must have been quite a refreshing change for Rosemary, who was more accustomed to clients who fussed over controlling costs. Even Prince Charles constantly wrote and admonished her to keep expenses down. Woodside would provide handsome fees for Rosemary.

Rosemary recalled the day Elton John's personal assistant called her in 1987 and mentioned Woodside. Rosemary observed, "The decision as to whether or not you can say 'yes' to a prospective client is often difficult." When she first heard the name Woodside, she recalled a mid-eighteenth-century rococo garden of the same name and found the reference in John Harris's book, *Gardens of Delight* (published in 1978), complete with watercolor illustrations of the 1750s. In typical fashion, she found a limited edition in America, which she bought and gave to Elton.[1]

She heard nothing further until 1988. Just as she was leaving on another trip to America, she was asked for a detailed garden plan "almost at once." Given the magnitude of the project and the demands of a deadline, Rosemary wisely realized she could not drop everything and take on Woodside. She probably could tell that its scale was far too ambitious for her to handle alone, especially since she had no garden design staff. And perhaps she instinctively sensed the client would prove mercurial in his tastes. Instead, she turned to Gordon Taylor and Guy Cooper, freelance garden designers, to oversee the project.

Ultimately, a big team was assembled – landscape designers, architects, full-time gardeners, Elton John's staff, and many others. It was orchestrated more like a corporate enterprise or the production company for a major show, with countless meetings, followed by written minutes to ensure all the work was coordinated. Rosemary wisely described herself as an "advisor," with particular responsibility for the choice of plants. In a draft of one set of minutes circulated to the participants, she was noted as the person responsible for producing "a scheme for winter plantings." In her quick correction, she noted her job was "not a scheme – just plants."[2]

Over the following years, Rosemary did create a design for specific areas of the garden. First, she designed a white garden just outside the drawing room doors of the main house. It was classic Rosemary, with carefully shaped beds outlined in box and filled with a profusion of white flowers she intended to be visible from the house, even in the faint light of early evening. "The French windows of the drawing room open on to a stone-paved terrace, and Elton told me that this was where he would entertain his friends on summer evenings. A white garden would provide the perfect setting for spring and summer parties. It was to be a peaceful place, a restful interlude among the variety of themes incorporated in the whole garden. . . . Elton would look down on this from his bedroom and walk into it from his drawing room. I love symmetry, and believe that for a garden beside the house where you entertain the borders should be curving, without awkward, acute corners."[3]

White gardens were very much *à la mode* following Vita Sackville-West's famous creation at Sissinghurst, and Rosemary gave her credit for the concept with its palette of white, greens, and grays. Her white garden for Elton John consisted principally of herbaceous flowering plants – ones that would take time to mature and settle in before looking their best. But time requires patience, a quality in short supply in the temperament of a fast-moving rock star accustomed to instant gratification of every shifting mood.

More positively, Rosemary described Elton John as "an enthusiast. He doesn't take a huge part [in the planning], he doesn't dig. He hasn't got time to dig. He is about the most energetic person that I possibly know."[4] During her first four years working at Woodside, Rosemary remarked that

Elton John was absent at least half the time, traveling on tour, giving concerts, and producing new albums. But she admired the fact that "he is a perfectionist, which is really good," a quality she certainly shared.

Anticipating a fleeting Christmas visit in 1993, Rosemary arranged to have a large number of white cyclamen specially grown. Just before his arrival at Woodside for the holidays and before he rushed away, she collected these special white cyclamen and drove them "briskly down to Windsor," working with the gardeners to quickly plant them. One wonders if Elton John fully took in these delicate, small white flowers, even with masses of them blooming outside his door.

Unfortunately, just as the white garden was coming into its own after three or four years, Elton John decided to rip it all out. He had been to Italy to visit his friend, the designer Gianni Versace and he suddenly decided he had to have an Italian garden. As was her habit, Rosemary had called upon her own entourage to help at Woodside, including Roy Strong. Possibly because Sir Roy was also a friend of Versace's, Elton asked him to do the design. When he was shown the area intended for the new garden, Roy said, "I can't do an Italian garden here. It's ridiculous. There's only one place to do it, here by this façade with the French windows." The same spot as Rosemary's white garden. When Roy pointed this out, Elton John replied, "Oh don't worry about that. We'll put a bulldozer through it," and Roy thought, "Oh my God, she'll never speak to me again!"[5]

While Rosemary could be ferocious in fighting for what was hers, she was uncharacteristically gracious to Roy Strong when he told her about this decision to bulldoze her garden. "She just sent the plans to me and wished me luck and I thought that was very, very big-spirited." He proceeded to rip out every last vestige of her white garden.

Instead he installed something quite imposing in its place. "I did a kind of arcade of busts of Roman Emperors, four statues of satyrs playing instruments. I don't think that was her style at all." In Sir Roy's view, men and women create different types of gardens, with men favoring stronger structures and women being "quite close focused. It's the men who do the big bold things."

If Roy Strong thought Rosemary was being generous about his obliteration, she certainly wasn't happy. She complained to her friends, observing "if Elton John wanted an Italian garden, why didn't he buy a house in Italy?!"[6] She did try to dissuade Elton John who turned a deaf ear to her plea to "please pause awhile before you take away the white garden. It has been successful since its first year and is now established."[7] Writing again after the deed was done, she said it "certainly is a change to Elton's original plan – I hope he likes it – it is certainly very formal and Italian – but is it Woodside?!?"[8]

Rosemary must have been furious, but she continued to be polite in public. No doubt she wanted to remain in Elton John's good graces and to continue to work for him. In her book *Rosemary Verey's Good Planting Plans*, which came out in 1993, Rosemary includes a piece about Woodside, but questions whether an Italian garden goes with the architecture of the house. Later, in her last book, *The English Country Garden*, she noted, "Sadly (for me), Elton decided he wanted an Italian garden, so after six years my white garden has gone, statues and vistas have taken over. I wonder, does an Italian garden blend with and complement an English Regency house?"

Clearly she was cross, but it was in her self-interest to be gracious. Possibly she wrote him directly to try to change his mind, but it seems likely that her displeasure failed to register.

Possibly it was blocked by the filter of his many other handlers and it may never even have reached his attention. Whether it did or not, her white garden was gone.

Even though her white garden had been eradicated, Rosemary continued to work at Woodside. Not only was the pay the highest she had ever earned, but her own reputation was enhanced by contact with a star client. She designed what she called the Ribbon Borders, which were gently shaped perennial borders planted in a harmonious range of colors in the style of Gertrude Jekyll, with one section of color harmoniously blending in to the next shade of the rainbow. Because Rosemary preferred softer pastels, she did not include the bolder and hotter colors that would have been included in a Jekyll border. She also helped create a potager for Woodside and contributed to the design of a developing woodland and cottage garden.

Always happiest when working with talented gardeners, Rosemary appreciated the skillful work of Elton John's head gardener, Helen Finch. Eventually, Rosemary expanded the herbaceous borders until they were fifty-five yards long and quite deep, with invisible paths running diagonally into the beds to allow access for maintenance. These borders, intended to offer interest throughout the season, demanded constant attention, and Rosemary clearly recognized the skill and work required to achieve this effect. "This style of planting . . . needs much skilled upkeep and a knowledge of the habit of plants, otherwise it becomes untidy and lacking in finesse when it should be brimming with ordered interest."[9]

While Rosemary enjoyed directing the work of talented gardeners, she was not used to taking orders herself or fitting into a team: she was used to being the boss. That was not the case at Woodside. The white garden episode was symptomatic. Much as Rosemary enjoyed basking in Elton John's fame, her work at Woodside cannot have been entirely satisfying. A small example of what must have been her ongoing irritation was a note written on a plan for the Woodside potager. Drawn up by Messers. Cooper and Taylor, who had placed their name at the bottom as the "creators," it impelled Rosemary to write in her firm hand the words "drawn by" in front of "Messrs. Cooper and Taylor," to clearly indicate that was their sole role. *She* was the creator.

Perhaps the most dramatic part of Woodside is the water garden, although Rosemary preferred to call it the scented garden. Inspired by the "famous fountain canal at the Generalife in Granada, with its arching water jets,"[10] the scented garden features a long narrow rill with fountains spouting across the center from either side, the end marked by a handsome garden pavilion. Huge pots, spilling over with a profusion of flowers, line the pavement running along each side of the rill, later surrounded by scented borders enclosed by trelliswork. Because this too was probably a team effort, there was a bit of a dust-up when Rosemary claimed credit for its design in her book *Rosemary Verey's Good Planting Plans*. Given its strong architectural elements, it is not a typical Rosemary Verey design, but since its true authorship was never established, nothing much came of this flap. It was just part of the ongoing high drama associated with working for Elton John.

Always drawing much publicity, Elton John's gardens appeared in numerous newspaper and magazine stories. One newspaper article about his rock garden had a headline that screamed "He's Lord of the Manor in 1 Million Pound Paradise."[11] No stranger to publicity and self-promotion herself, Rosemary often wrote to Elton John asking to use his garden in some presentation she wanted to give, seeking a short quote from him or his permission to have television cameras arrive to film her there. He was usually generous in granting these requests.

Rosemary was wise to avoid taking charge at Woodside because she continued to be very busy with work on other fronts and with her books. In 1989, *The Flower Arranger's Garden* appeared, followed by two more books at the beginning in 1990, *The American Man's Garden* and *Good Planting*.

The Flower Arranger's Garden is not a how-to-arrange-flowers book at all. Instead, it offers practical advice about planning a garden with enough flowers throughout the seasons to both fill the house and allow the garden to continue looking beautiful. Rosemary emphasizes the need for careful planning to achieve this. "Skill includes making sure the flowers that are in bloom simultaneously have matching, blending or complementary colours,"[12] but she also emphasizes the use of leaves and branches. In order to keep the garden looking lovely, "you cannot afford to be self-indulgent and devote a large space to a plant which is ravishingly, but fleetingly, beautiful in flower." Then she goes on to encourage her reader not to hesitate to pick garden flowers. "Above all, if you are a gardener, disabuse yourself of the idea that it is a sin to rob the garden to adorn the house. With thought and enthusiastic planting you can do both."

The book is full of admonitions to be thoughtful and plan carefully, as well as to observe colors as they alter in different light. "As with everything in life, success lies in method. I cannot emphasize too much or too often how important it is to plan ... to make the most of every month, I suggest that you make a chart of what you need and what will be available at each time of year." As always, she urges her readers to use a notebook to record attractive combinations and build up a list of desirable plants. "You think you will remember them, but I can guarantee that you won't." The book then provides useful plans for borders in multiple seasons and describes in detail sixty-four useful plants. The book is enhanced by photographs of luscious flower arrangements in various styles, almost all of which were created for the book by the photographer, Linda Burgess.

Good Planting, or in America, *The Art of Planting*, with exquisite photographs by Andrew Lawson, is a more substantive book. It is not clear who chose the American title, but it is exactly the same as one used earlier by Graham Stuart Thomas in his book that came out in England and the United States in 1984. But then Rosemary often admitted she drew heavily on what had come before. In *Good Planting*, Rosemary analyzes her thoughts about why some of her combinations worked beautifully, while others, despite careful calculation, didn't work. She writes about pleasing all the senses "to satisfy our eyes and agitate our hearts." Comparing a gardener to a painter, she perceives that "in some ways, (the gardener's) task is more complex, since his palette is composed not only of living colours, but also of changing textures, and his canvas is fluid in time – maturing, fading, finally ceasing to exist."[13]

Trial and error are encouraged. "Good planting skills are not abstract concepts to be learnt solely from books, catalogues and other people. The best way to start is by learning to look, and in looking to see and to see critically." Rosemary herself was prone to picking a particular flower and then carrying it around her garden to hold up against other plants then in bloom in order to think about possible planting combinations. Quoting Diogenes as saying "Nothing costs us so dear as a waste of time," she adds, "but never think that moments spent walking round your garden are wasted time. In them the seed of inspiration may be sown, and without inspiration a garden may be pretty but lack beauty, interesting but not memorable, and disturbing rather than restful. Ideas take time to evolve and mature, and it is by sitting or walking silently that they can come flooding in."

The book includes chapters on Colour, Shape and Texture, Bulbs, Herbaceous Borders, Mixed Borders, Climbers and Wall Shrubs, Ground Cover and Low Maintenance Plants, Woodland, Wild Areas and Damp Sites, and Tubs and Containers. Its text is full of her advice and encouragement to the reader to develop their own skills and taste. Recognizing that once a garden is in place, it is hard to look at it with a critical eye, she encourages the reader not only to look critically at their own garden, but to visit others, as always advocating to "keep a notebook in your pocket or a camera in your car." She suggests that even fabrics can be a source of inspiration for color combinations. Here too the book includes several possible planting plans.

Rosemary also carried on design work for others, including the Marquess of Bute, who gave her the perfect assignment. He asked her to advise him on the future of a large, walled garden at Mount Stuart, his home on the island of Bute, just off the west coast of Scotland. Even though it was quite a long trip to get there, Rosemary was fortunate to be able to call upon her good friends, Vic and Anne Norman, who often flew her there in their small plane. Working with the very able head gardener, Paul Martin, Rosemary produced some lovely plans for six well-defined areas, with the first priority given to vegetables, along with spaces for a cutting garden, herbs, and fruit. She viewed the growing of flowers and vegetables together as consistent with Scottish tradition, but she insisted this was "not a 'set piece' – rather, to make a twentieth century equivalent, conscious of historical and philosophical precedents. Nor is an essay on nostalgia the aim!"[14]

The design work and her other writings were carried out simultaneously while Rosemary continued her work at Woodside over many years. The mercurial tastes of Elton John meant that the gardens changed frequently. New features were constantly added, new ideas installed to replace prior work. Statues and structures multiplied. Although she had no hand in it, Rosemary shared Elton's wicked delight when a fake dinosaur arrived as a gift from George Harrison. At first, the dinosaur sat in the middle of a central lawn until it was taken by helicopter and moved to lurk in the Woodland. Rosemary thought this airborne trip "must have been a bit of a shock, and now she duly responds by surprising unknowing visitors, especially after dark when an infra-red sensor is automatically set to light her up."[15] This dinosaur, with its eyes flashing, continues to terrify unsuspecting strollers who inadvertently trip the switch.

Despite Elton John's deep pockets and big budgets, Messrs. Cooper and Taylor went into liquidation and ended up in a messy dispute with him about their fees. Since Rosemary submitted her bills through them, she too was affected. As a result of an eventual settlement, Rosemary's outstanding bills of roughly £32,000 yielded only £12,000, and because this settlement was handled by Elton's general managers, it is not clear how much Elton knew of its unfortunate impact on Rosemary. Still, the fees she received from her work at Woodside were far more substantial than those she normally charged. Quite often, her payments were sent directly into accounts for her grandchildren's education.

For his fiftieth birthday party, Elton John threw an enormous bash, and Rosemary was invited.[16] Everyone was asked to come in costume and Elton John's outfit was – predictably – outrageously flamboyant. He arrived as a fantasy version of Louis XIV, a vision of white and silver. His white wig of curls towered several feet over his head, topped by a tall silver ornament. He wore a white sequined jacket and knee breeches, white silk stockings, and silver high-heeled shoes, wrapped in a flowing, floor-length cloak swathed in white feathers. The costume was so elaborate and heavy he could barely walk. A large truck carried him into the party.

Escorted by her friend, Arthur Reynolds, Rosemary arrived dressed as a flower border. More demure than Elton, her flower borders were part of the printed pattern on her dress. Arthur describes the scene as being exactly what one would expect for a rock star's birthday party. The crowd was huge, the music electrifying and overpowering, the energy infectious. Rosemary, nearly eighty, had no trouble fitting in. She always loved a party and, as usual, was among the last to leave. "Seeing her at parties, she was like a child, a teenage girl. So much energy, flitting from one conversation to another. Roaring with laughter. Great fun. Wonderful sense of fun."[17] When asked afterwards how she found Elton's party, she said merely, "Terribly loud!"[18]

While Rosemary was working for Elton John, another royal client appeared, this one a real king. Rosemary was asked to help in the gardens of King Hussein of Jordan and Queen Noor at their property called Buckhurst Park in Ascot, not far from Woodside. Rosemary loved her work at Buckhurst, and it carried on over a period of several years. She wrote numerous letters of advice on a wide range of topics, from the choice of roses to long lists of plants for the herbaceous borders, along with the names of nurseries from which to order them.

In one letter, she laid out her views about designing gardens. "Gardening is very much an ongoing creation. Whereas interior decorators can 'do' curtains and chintzes to make an immediate and impressive impact, these will slowly become less crisp; settle into middle age and then need replacing. Your garden, however, with a sound structure should develop each year and will be [your] intrinsic enjoyment . . . [but do] not expect a mature effect this 'June'."[19]

And to the gardener who was responsible for maintaining the Buckhurst garden, she advised, "It is vitally important that your greenhouse staff must always supply you with sufficient plants to use in the main gardens. Forward planning is vital regarding this!"[20] She enjoyed the team there. The head gardener was respectful and appreciative of her advice rather than being proprietary or competitive. Rosemary especially enjoyed working for the King and Queen.

As usual in her design work, Rosemary called upon her own gardeners and garden allies for support. Rosemary sent Margie Hoffnung, who had worked at Barnsley in 1991, to find out why the Buckhurst gardens weren't developing according to plan. Nothing seemed to be happening there. Margie reported back. "It was clear there were all sorts of staffing problems. There was one very nice old boy but the other gardener was very disruptive, didn't really do any work or pull his weight. Sadly, the good man was then fired." Even more sadly, Rosemary's work at Buckhurst came to an abrupt halt when King Hussein died.[21]

For all her success, it was not until 1991 that Rosemary was asked to design a show garden for the Chelsea Flower Show, the summit of gardening events. She had once before participated in the creation of a garden for Chelsea but only in a minor role. In 1985, she had selected the varieties of fruit trees for a Chelsea garden of fruits and herbs designed and installed by Highfield Nursery. She had not done anything for Chelsea since and never had her own showcase. But the *Evening Standard* asked her to design a garden that they would sponsor for the Show scheduled for the spring of

1992. Many of her friends and extended cast of supporting characters pitched in to help with this challenging undertaking. Her New York friend Victor Nelson came over to help along with many others. John Hill was right there to work on the hardscaping and prepare the formal plans, which had to be submitted to the Royal Horticultural Society for approval well in advance of installation.

Rosemary and John Hill had no idea how to do this. They treated this assignment as if they were designing a permanent garden for a client, intended to endure forever, rather than for a week's display at Chelsea. John recalls, "We'd never done a show at Chelsea Gardens. We made it exactly as if we were making a proper garden. It would have lasted for a hundred years."

Rosemary called it a Town Garden, but in many ways, it was a "small version of her garden at home."[22] It was typical of Rosemary to hope that "visitors would look around and feel inspired by some of the ideas we included – that they might say to each other 'We can do this at home', or 'This is a great idea for our garden.'"[23]

The garden had box edging and sharply defined flowerbeds interspersed with brick and stone paths. A charming conservatory was installed, along with a grotto, replicating in a small way the grotto Rosemary had at The Close. Beautiful pots were planted by Rupert Golby (who would go on to win Gold at Chelsea himself for the show gardens he later created there). An obligatory statue by Simon Verity enhanced the scene; Rosemary lent her own statue of the Lady Gardener for the purpose. The garden's gates were painted the same special blue as those in front of the Barnsley temple, and the plantings included all of Rosemary's favorites, including her scented herbs. Even the arches intended to display hanging gourds were identical to her Barnsley potager, but because Chelsea takes place in May, no fall maturing gourds could be featured.

Perhaps it was a sign of the beginning of the end of Rosemary's reign that she won merely a Silver, not the coveted Gold. The garden was very well received by the public, but the "judges were sniffy that it wasn't 'innovative.' The planting was vintage Rosemary Verey. It wasn't ground breaking. No new ideas. Traditional."[24] Being as competitive as she was, her Silver Medal was a disappointment. Rosemary would never design a garden for Chelsea again.

CHAPTER TEN

Love Affair with America
1990s

Here in America you all want to know, you listen,
I love your enthusiasm.[1]

OSEMARY'S LOVE AFFAIR with America probably began on her first visit, but it was certainly solidified by the books she later wrote about American gardens. At the start of the 1990s, her book *The American Man's Garden* came out, based on the same successful format as her earlier *The American Woman's Garden* and the original *The Englishwoman's Garden* and *The Englishman's Garden*. This time, however, Rosemary was the sole author, although she acknowledges it was written in association with Katherine Lambert, her long-time personal assistant. The American garden writer Allen Lacy observes in the foreword that these two books about American gardens are "particularly useful in correcting the false notion that many Americans have about our horticulture's being vastly inferior to that of Great Britain."[2]

Americans in turn adored her for validating their own gardening vernacular. The books gave her a special link, since everyone included in the book, and many who helped with them, would be sure to welcome her whenever her travels took her anywhere near their vicinity. They were proud to have been selected as creators of special American gardens, and all were eager to fete her, generously hosting parties in her honor. These men and women formed a dedicated core of fans, but they were just a small fraction of her ever-expanding American network. In her own acknowledgements in *The American Man's Garden*, Rosemary thanks a long list of people with whom she has stayed and others who have taken her around their gardens. It is a *Who's Who* of Americans, not only of American gardeners.

Reflecting her extensive American travels, *The American Man's Garden* includes essays from twenty-nine men with gardens in eighteen states, from the East to the West Coast and several states in between, including one in Vancouver, Canada. The essays written by the garden owners are grouped under the following categories: estate gardens; country gardens; plant collectors; city and town; poets and painters; and seaside, mountain, desert. In a lengthy introduction, Rosemary draws upon her interest in garden history and links American garden development to the early English settlers who carried plants and garden notions with them to the New World. And she generously gives credit to American plantsmen like the Bartrams of Philadelphia who sent native seeds and plants to England, changing the face of British gardens.

Bill Frederick recalls that she managed to make everyone in the book feel good. Since his own garden was pictured on the frontispiece of *The American Man's Garden*, he certainly had reason to be grateful, but he appreciated how delicate her role had been with everyone involved. Bill understood that "People could easily take offense if one didn't get the same amount of attention as the other one or didn't get as many kudos or whatever. She achieved that by really being good at picking out the positive aspects of each person and each garden that she went to, so each one became different." Her inscription to Bill on his personal copy of the book says, "For Bill and Nancy – the best garden is on page 142. I discovered once and for all that every visit is more and more magical."

A knowledgeable and professional plantsman himself, Bill thought Rosemary had a rare ability to take in what she saw and "was one of the people that understood the kind of design that I was doing, and other Americans, better than any British person that's ever been around here." Not surprisingly, given her early university studies in social history, she "could adapt immediately to whatever the local conditions were and, to some extent, to the sociological aspects, the history of the area that the garden was in, especially if the garden was reflecting that." She paid attention to what worked in each locality.

Following one of her fundamental rules, she always had paper and pencil in hand, noting the plants along with her observations. Unlike most other British gardening experts who came to America with "their usual palette of plants,"[3] she did her homework and worked hard to learn which plants would work in the climate and conditions of the place where she was visiting. And if she promised to send seeds, as she often did, she always delivered.

Rosemary's timing could not have been better. In the 1980s and 1990s, Americans were developing an increasing sophistication and interest in all things international, although most were initially modest about their own abilities. Americans looked to England to set the standards for great garden style. While there were those who emulated Japanese and Chinese gardens, and others who loved the formal structures of Italian gardens, Rosemary appealed to the vast majority of American gardeners who looked first and foremost to England for their models, but she encouraged them to think Americans were fully capable of creating their own garden aesthetic. "She was just there at the right time. You know when people were ready for all these lovely books. And she had the garden to show and of course her garden was also on the tourist circuit. It was plum there in the Cotswolds where all the Americans and other tourists passed through. So she was perfectly placed geographically, as well as historically."[4]

The fact that Rosemary Verey, the quintessential British lady, chose to feature American gardens as worthy of attention endeared her to a primed and receptive constituency. More importantly, her books showed Americans how much their countrymen and women already knew about creating memorable gardens, and she admired them. Tom Cooper, editor of *Horticulture* magazine, thought she was a "charming speaker. She made it a personal conversation in a very friendly way. She was very intimate. She admitted errors and it all felt very much like an honest account. You weren't being lectured to, you were having a conversation with her."

Rosemary's American travel schedule each year built on the links she created through her books, especially her two books on American gardens. She usually went several times each year, covering great distances from coast to coast, with many stops in between. She became a regular in the Pacific Northwest, especially for the Northwest Flower and Garden Show, which began in 1989 and took place in Seattle in February of each year. Occasionally it was also held in nearby Vancouver, British Columbia. Next to Philadelphia's, the Northwest Show quickly became the nation's largest flower show.

Dan Hinkley, plant explorer extraordinaire and founder of the renowned nursery, Heronswood, just outside Seattle, observed that "gardening really was at a fever pitch when Rosemary was at her height . . . especially in the Northwest here, which tends to be one of the centers of horticultural snobbery in the States. There was just an amazing devotion to the English mixed border. And trying to make it the American border. All the people were going to England to buy plants and bring them back. And she was sort of the bridge between American and English horticulture for a long time."[5] She often spoke at the Northwest Flower Show and when she did, "she fortified our self-esteem, compared our gardening to that going on in Britain and often implied that we were doing it better in the Northwest."[6]

Dan was impressed by Rosemary's endless curiosity and her interest in local culture. Whenever she was in Seattle, she would "often go to the black Baptist Churches on Sunday. She loved the Pentecostals, the singing, the holy rollers." He also enjoyed her sense of humor. Although she was not generally given to telling jokes, she could elicit laughs herself. One time Dan Hinkley picked her up outside of Seattle from the ferry in his pickup truck. Since he had just been carting horse manure in it, he said, "Rosemary, I really apologize for not having brought the other car. I brought this pick-up, and it's had horse manure in it. And she came back without batting an eyelash, 'Oh shit!'"

Gregory Long remembers this as "a moment in time. Garden photographers certainly helped put her on the map and Rosemary's books were everywhere. As America wasn't producing many of its own gardening books, its gardening books came from England." And her books sold extraordinarily well in the States, often exceeding 50,000 copies. For several books, Rosemary received from her London publisher, Frances Lincoln, a £40,000 advance, a staggering sum for the time.[7]

As Gregory Long recalls, "She loved being a celebrity." He felt that in America "everyone here needed her, they needed her books. They had real content, they were not just lovely photographs; you could learn from them. They were written by a very intelligent voice that could talk to an American audience and they weren't just about the gardens of the wealthy." Barnsley was not a grand estate. So it was relevant to ordinary people, and she perceived that relevance. As a result, Gregory felt her message was clearly that "You can make gardens like mine, borders like mine, containers like mine; you can learn how to make a Laburnum Arch like mine."

Ryan Gainey, an American garden designer based in Atlanta, "always thought she was much better known here than she was in England." In America, "she was contagious. Because you know how Americans are about the English. And how they just love to hear an English person speak, it just lifts them up. She just simply came on the scene when there was a great revolution in gardening in America. And somebody had to be the one and she became it. She was totally socially astute and gracious and very thoughtful toward everybody. And people loved having her around. She integrated herself into the idea of American gardening through *The American Woman's Garden* and *The American Man's Garden*. She had the personality that could take what she had learned on her own and teach Americans who were struggling."

Ryan Gainey introduced her to his own client and Atlanta-based neighbor, Anne Cox Chambers, who owned Le Petit Fontanille, a lovely home in St. Rémy, Provence, France, with gardens covering over forty acres, almost twelve acres of which are formal ornamental gardens. Rosemary thought the outlines, which had been designed by her friend Peter Coats, were good, but that the garden needed some reviving.

Rosemary worked on various parts of the garden with Ryan Gainey. Serge Pauleau, the head gardener at Le Petit Fontanille for over twenty years, who oversees five full-time gardeners, recalled that Rosemary worked on an ornamen-

tal potager there and also decided to create a cutting garden: "Mrs. Verey designed that cutting garden and took the
pattern from a book." While she did produce a rough sketch,
she followed her preference for laying the shapes and plants
out on the ground. It has her usual geometric patterns, filled
with flowers useful for indoor arrangements. Perhaps her
biggest contribution to Anne Cox Chambers was to suggest
she hire Tim Rees. Tim became a major force in the ongoing development of the gardens, adding strong outdoor
rooms and rich tapestries of plantings.

When Anne Cox Chambers later invited Rosemary to a
dinner party in Atlanta, she commissioned an extraordinary
centerpiece for the table. It was a replica of the Barnsley
potager, measuring eight feet long and three feet wide. Mrs.
Chambers flew the florist who created this centerpiece in
from New York – the plants were all live![8]

Rosemary loved this sort of American extravagance; she
was treated like a star or better still, royalty, wherever she
went. While she enjoyed enthusiastic gardeners of any and
all stripes, she was clearly happiest when in the company of
the rich and famous, such as Oscar de la Renta. He was
beginning to establish his own impressive garden in the
northwestern corner of Connecticut with some structural
advice from Russell Page. Rosemary was asked to write an
article about Oscar's garden for *House & Garden* magazine
and made a date to go see it. Although Oscar planned to
meet her in his garden, a storm prevented him arriving in
time. Despite his own position, Oscar admitted to her afterwards, "I was so unbelievably relieved . . . because I was
absolutely terrified!"[9] She in turn replied that she had woken
up worrying about what to wear to meet the great designer,
saying, "Shall I wear my pink skirt and my white blouse?"
They did finally meet in New York, and Oscar succumbed to

her charms. She told him she had written in her diary, "Today I met a man and I think we are going to become very good friends."

Oscar joined her long list of American admirers and soon he was giving her some of his expensive designer clothes as gifts. After she thanked him for some of the clothes he had given her, he replied, "I hope you'll be a big hit in them. You are the new Oscar de la Renta glamour girl!"[10] Oscar enjoyed "her feminine quality. Even in her old age, she could be flirtatious." He responded to her warmth and astutely observed that "if she liked someone, and I don't think she liked everybody, but if she liked someone, you really felt it. She had a magnetic force. She was a force of nature. Something strong, but not manly. Something very coquettish about her. She had tenacity, and an intensity and a passion." Rosemary never designed a garden for Oscar, but she offered advice and was quite forceful in her views, advising him to take out a line of roses he had planted under an allée of trees to open the view.

With so much travel and design work, some of Rosemary's close friends and observers thought she was coasting a bit in her writing, capitalizing on her brand but without living up to her usual high standards. Indeed, two of her books, *The Garden Gate* in 1991 and *A Gardener's Book of Days* in 1992, appear to be purely commercial affairs. The first was a small book in a series; it required her to write nothing more than a short introduction with short captions to pages of photographs of garden gates shown in various styles and settings. The second book was nothing more than a glorified calendar, with a short essay about each month and then empty pages for entries of dates and notes.

A Countrywoman's Notes also came out in 1991 and though it is a charming book, it also required little work on Rosemary's part. There was nothing original in it. The book was produced by Rosemary's daughter Davina Wynne-Jones and was a compilation of some of her best of *Country Life*, selected from her columns written between 1979 and 1987 when Rosemary ceased writing for the magazine.[11] The extracts are grouped by the months of a year and adorned with handsome engravings produced by a dozen artists. The topics are more about nature and life in the country over the course of the year than horticulture and cover a broad range from whippets, to bee swarms, to local Gloucestershire history.

As a remarkable tribute to their friendship, Prince Charles stated in the foreword that "Mrs. Verey . . . makes gardening seem the easiest and most natural thing in the world." He goes on to say, "The garden at Barnsley House (which I love and you must visit) comes to life." And then he puts Rosemary very much in the context of the Arts and Crafts movement, saying that "Mrs. Verey reveres the world of Ernest Gimson and Sidney Barnsley, those dedicated Arts and Crafts practitioners from nearby Sapperton. They would have approved so much of these wonderful wood engravings whose depth is such a good medium for revealing the intricacies of hedgerows. And wouldn't William Morris have approved from across the willowy meadows in Kelmscott?" After a beautiful house, the next thing to be longed for, he said, was a "Beautiful Book. Here is one." And then he signs "Charles."[12] A valuable endorsement not only of the book but of Rosemary and her gardens at Barnsley.

In the spring of 1994, Rosemary joined Christopher Lloyd for a lecture tour across America. Although they knew each other, Rosemary had not been Christopher Lloyd's first choice. He had intended to travel with Beth Chatto, his close friend and a superb plantswoman, with her own specialty nursery and gardens in Essex. Christopher Lloyd, or "Christo," as he was called by his friends, and Beth Chatto shared a passion for plants and swapped ideas and advice, some of which resulted in a book of their letters to each other.[13] Unfortunately, Beth Chatto's husband became seriously ill and she felt she couldn't leave him, so Rosemary stepped into the breach.

At first Rosemary and Christo must have seemed an unlikely couple, but they proved to be a terrific team. They were "very supportive and cordial, but with quite a bit of good-humored barbing. They were caricatures in a way. Rosemary was this stylish Liberty of London with a high-pitched, elegant voice and Christopher was this gruff, marbles-in-his-mouth creature."[14] The two of them played off each other's foibles, with Christopher making fun of her polite pastel palette and Rosemary joking about his messy ways. At one lecture, she spoke first and showed a diagram of the color wheel as a point of reference. Christo purported not to understand it. When his turn came to show slides of his garden's radical color combinations of magenta and orange, he teased, "You can see that I've never followed the color wheel."[15] Their banter amused their audiences and their shared seriousness about plants and gardens drew them into a strong friendship. They were certainly equals.

During their tour, Rosemary and Christo had dinner at Tom Cooper's home in Boston. After a long, tiring day that would have exhausted anyone, Rosemary was still fresh and completely at ease, "just gay and happy and friendly."[16] She plunked Tom's young daughter up on the kitchen counter and chatted away with her in the most natural manner. Somewhat flustered by his famous guests, Tom completely forgot to start cooking the wild rice in time, scrambling to find a quick substitute. As part of the conversation at dinner, Rosemary praised Prime Minister Margaret Thatcher for restoring "the upper classes which were in decline," and for "giving the aristocracy back a sense of itself, for giving the Royals back a sense of themselves."[17] Although not terribly political, she tended to be conservative and a strong supporter of the royal family. Katherine Lambert, Rosemary's assistant who was traveling with her and had more liberal views, jumped in to disagree, pointing out the unemployment problems and other inequities. After Katherine had gone on for awhile, Rosemary looked round the table, then back to Katherine and "very sweetly but very steely said, 'Katherine. If you continue in this manner when we get back to the hotel, I shall have to strike you!'" Although she purported to be joking, Tom was sure she meant it.

The evening ended after far too much scotch, and as Rosemary and Christo left, stumbling off in the direction of a waiting taxi, Rosemary stopped, looked back, and swirled her arms at two far-too-large hemlocks towering over the front porch and shouted back to Tom, "You must do topiaries! Topiaries!"

A day later, Tom drove Rosemary and Christo to stay with Joe Eck and Wayne Winterrowd, at their plant-intensive garden, North Hill, in Vermont. On the way, she talked very openly about her need to earn a lot of money for herself and her family, along with her concerns about the future of Barnsley and its gardens. Christo snored away in the back. Tom felt she was not just seeking his sympathy, but was clearly wrestling with these issues.

They arrived at the height of black fly season and Joe and Wayne warned Rosemary to cover herself with bug repellant before going out with them to see the garden. In the process of having herself sprayed, she was outrageously flirtatious with all the attentive men, later observing, "I could never have done this when David was around."

That observation was quite revealing. In America, Rosemary

clearly enjoyed being free from many of the constraints she felt at home. "She allowed herself a measure of play and certainly of freedom that she could never have allowed herself at home." Her good friend, Andrew Lawson, observed that although she wasn't herself aristocracy, she "was very grand and she got on well with the grand . . . in style she associated herself with the aristocracy. The Americans are completely unaware of all these things where the English are always very aware. As soon as she was in the American context she was free, free of all those things. And [the Americans] all made such a fuss about her and she loved it."

She was also endlessly curious about things American and always fearless. On a visit to Harlem in New York City, she went happily into a leather shop that sold jackets. Her American companion suggested she shouldn't go in because it was a "black" store, to which she blithely replied, "What does it matter?" She entered and bought herself a motorcycle biker's jacket with multi-colored patches of leather and a cap to go with it. Afterwards, she boldly sported this outfit at home in Cirencester, despite her age.[18] She also proved to be an enthusiastic Texas two-stepper, delighting in dancing late into the night with her American friend, Victor Nelson. And because she was not constrained by American conventions, she could be very direct. At one dinner party, she turned to her host and asked him point blank, "Now tell me, are you a millionaire or a billionaire?" His somewhat surprised reply was "Actually, I'm a billionaire."

One of Rosemary's proudest American moments occurred on August 13, 1994. Never having completed her university degree, Rosemary received an honorary doctorate in humane letters from the University of South Carolina at their summer commencement. In the photograph of the event, she looks happy and dignified in her academic robe and soft cap with a gold tassel. She thought this was "an important moment in my life," and was delighted that the other honoree was a colleague "of Martin Luther King."[19] More than just a Martin Luther King colleague, the other honoree was Andrew Young, who was Mayor of Atlanta, a Congressman, and the first African American to serve as American ambassador to the United Nations, among many other achievements.

Americans bought her books in huge numbers and also sought her advice. Sometimes it was an informal consultation, but there were serious assignments as well. If she so much as offered a suggestion, the garden owner forever after would boast of having a "Rosemary Verey" garden.

One of her serious assignments was for Richard and Sheila Sanford, who asked her to help them design ambitious gardens around the stone Cotswold-style manor house they were building in the Brandywine Valley just outside Wilmington, Delaware. The style of the house was very similar to Rosemary's own Barnsley, with stone lintels, leaded windows, and architectural details imported from England, but concealing the most modern fiber-optic technology in its walls. The house site was atop a hill overlooking the magnificent rolling countryside. The Sanfords' gardener, John Gallagher, suggested they call in an American, Neil Diboll, a wildflower expert, to help develop the meadows along winding drives throughout the extensive property. Because of Richard Sanford's interest in coaching, these drives were intended for horse-drawn carriage events. When Neil Diboll came, he suggested the Sanfords hire Rosemary Verey for the gardens.

In response to a letter from Neil Diboll, Rosemary came to meet the Sanfords while in Wilmington giving a lecture and staying with her good friend, Bill Frederick, who lived nearby. Although the Sanfords had been intimidated by her fame and were reluctant to ask for her attentions, they were quickly enchanted with her warm, down-to-earth manner. Rosemary enlisted Bill Frederick to help do the actual planting. In addition to her work on their garden, Rosemary also introduced the Sanfords to English suppliers who could provide Cotswold stone and other genuine English materials. While Bill Frederick and John Gallagher worked on developing the big picture, including long allées of trees to frame the striking views from the house to the distant landscape, Rosemary focused on the more formal plantings close to the house. Bill worked on the "overall concepts. Rosemary worked from the details up and [Bill] worked from concepts down."[20]

Two of the gardens she designed for the Sanfords were patterned on her own garden, one a knot garden, the other a large, walled potager. The potager still exists almost exactly as she designed it, dominated by a large, handsome stone building at one end. Richard Sanford remembers her insisting on a full-scale mockup created so the size and proportions of this building could be designed precisely for the setting. Given the imposing scale of the main house overlooking this potager below, it was a wise move. By trying out variations with a full-sized model, Rosemary ensured the garden folly would be proportioned exactly, large enough to be handsome but not so large as to overwhelm the potager or block the spectacular views beyond. Sheila Sanford has since become an accomplished gardener herself and keeps this potager true to her intentions; it remains one of the few gardens Rosemary designed that is still intact and complete.

The Sanfords also recall Rosemary's common sense and willingness to listen to them, along with her savvy and practical country solutions. The woodland nearest the Sanfords' house was overrun with multiflora rose and other invasive plants that had engulfed the handsome trees. No one had a good solution as to how to destroy these weeds without injuring the trees. State environmental laws prohibited the use of strong herbicides; bulldozing would be overkill. The weeds remained an eyesore, as well as a danger to the survival of the trees. One day, Richard Sanford said in passing to Rosemary, "How the heck do we get rid of that stuff?" Countrywoman that she was, Rosemary replied, "Have you thought about goats?" Astonished, Richard admitted goats had never occurred to him. He wasn't quite sure what she was getting at but goats proved the perfect solution. A herd of goats was purchased and set loose under the trees within the confines of a temporary fence. "It was like a carpet cleaner – Whoosh – they ate everything! They were just like weed eating machines!"[21] As the goats ate an area clean, the fence and goats were then moved on to the next overrun section and in short order, the beautiful stand of two hundred mature coffee trees was visible and the weeds were gone.

In the summer of 1997, the New York Botanical Garden commissioned her to design a potager along the lines of the famous one she had created at Barnsley. This was the only public garden she was ever asked to design and it was in America. Although this potager has not yet been built, the plans have been fully developed and the site chosen. From the start, Gregory Long made it clear that Rosemary's garden would not be installed until NYBG raised sufficient funds to build it as well as endow its ongoing maintenance. Ever a realist, Rosemary knew that Beatrix Farrand had designed a re - nowned rose garden for NYBG in 1916 that wasn't completed until 1988. She was confident that someday her potager would be installed, providing her a legacy in the United States. Perhaps that is why Rosemary ultimately chose to bequeath all her garden plans to the NYBG Library rather than an English institution.

When Gregory Long asked Rosemary to design this garden, he was puzzled as to why she had never been asked to
design a public garden in England. "We could never figure
it out. She was never asked to design a public garden there
and she was never on the Council [of the RHS]." Having
become a close personal friend of Rosemary's over the years,
Gregory and his partner, Scott Newman, often had Rosemary stay with them at their country house in upstate New
York. In turn, they also often visited Barnsley but chose not
to stay there. "She was sometimes too difficult, even cross,
and as we were quite intimate, she often told us more than
we wanted to know about her family relationships." But
when Rosemary came to stay with them in New York, she
seemed to shed all that. "She really could drop so much of
her baggage and jump into the moment. And when she came
to us she was quite relaxed, not needing to be in charge."

Rosemary's potager for NYBG had to be on a much larger
scale than her intimate one at home. It had to comply with
all the applicable building codes, provide accessibility, and
adapt to many other rules pertaining to a public facility.
Rosemary worked with a large team of professionals, including architects, administrators, and other horticultural experts
under the leadership of Dr. Kim Tripp, who at the time was
Vice President for Horticulture and later became Director,
and was herself an expert in conifers.

Everyone agrees that the designs are completely Rosemary's, but many other professionals participated, rather like
the large team that had worked with her at Elton John's.
They helped produce the architectural drawings and computerized files. The work dragged on over many months,
with Rosemary reviewing and revising the designs after they
were drawn to her specifications by professional architects
and draftsmen. Rosemary didn't particularly enjoy the disci-

pline of laying out all the lines with such precision, but she would leave her sketches, suggested notes, and revisions, and they would all be incorporated in the next computerized version produced by John Kirk, the architect from the firm of Cooper Robertson working on the project.

As always, her real love was in the planting plans. She relished "deciding where the cold crops would go over years 1, 3 and 5 and the lettuces would go in years 3, 5 and 7 and then she'd switch them to allow for the rotation of crops and make a list for year 1 and year 2."[22] Characteristically open to the local culture, Rosemary was interested in the Bronx community that was primarily Hispanic and African American. She learned about "Bronx Green-Up, and some of the vegetables that were grown by Latin American gardeners. She met with them a few times and put a few of those in because she thought this is the Bronx and some things of local interest would be good in the vegetable garden." Rosemary always paid attention to one of her basic rules, "Who is the audience and what is the message?" Here she made sure to include some ideas that would appeal to the neighbors.

Preferring to be hands on, Rosemary had the most fun working on this project when she was out in the garden. "She was dying to get out with the two gardeners on the ground with some open beds, lay out the hose and design the bed with the hose and start talking about which plants should go where." Kim Tripp thought she had a kind of "gardener radar"; she could spot the working gardeners in any group. Then she would be completely engaged with them, soaking up and listening to what they had to say while offering knowledge in return.

Although Rosemary liked best to be out on the site, she was thoroughly professional. "She came to the design work with enormous patience and intense concentration on every detail." To Kim Tripp, she was the antithesis of the "twenty-first-century instant CAD designer." Instead, she would "very painstakingly and attentively draw out and think about all these details so it all came together very beautifully." Kim Tripp found her an inspiration. She was the real thing. She could talk about the most minute aspects of the plants in great depth and detail. She knew every plant "like one of her children so that she knew when it had been nice and when it had been naughty."

Rosemary's attention to detail and her reworking of the plans with almost excruciating precision were impressive. Rosemary was "thoroughly committed to taking however much time it took to get to the right answer in the design. [For example] she would spend days thinking about and detailing paving patterns." Kim, a master multi-tasker, used to jumping quickly from one issue to the next, remembers being taken to task. "She would kind of look at me out of the corner of her eye with the twinkle when she could see that I was getting a little impatient about how long it was taking to figure out which corner this medallion should go in the paving and where exactly the step-over apples should end in relation to the radishes and then she'd look at me with that kind of expression, and I would realize that this really does matter, I should just not be worried about rushing off to do the next thing. She didn't have to say a word. She would just look at me with this certain kind of sparky look and I would know, okay, so I should stop jiggling my knee."

Rosemary could also grow testy. "Periodically she would get impatient with us." Simon Verity, whom Rosemary brought in to sculpt a piece for the potager, recalls moments when she was "being such a bitch. She just crucified poor Kim Tripp who was doing her utmost to be helpful. 'What are you doing? Why do you get involved at all?'" But Simon believes that her ill health was causing her to lose control. Even though she tried to carry on as usual, she was prone to lashing out in frustration when she wasn't up to it.

Indeed her health was beginning to fail toward the end of the decade. Rosemary thought she had fought off the threat of arthritis some years before when she consulted a nutritionist who recommended she avoid dairy products and wheat. But with age her energies began to flag and she was afflicted with polymyalgia rheumatism; as a result, she was often medicated for the pain.

But America continued to honor her. In October 1998, she went to Boston to receive the George Robert White Medal of Honor from the Massachusetts Horticultural Society. Her friend, Jerry Harpur, whom she enlisted to accompany her, recalls that at one point during her acceptance speech, she chose to tell her Boston audience that when David Verey had asked her to marry him, she had replied, "Yes, but I won't pick up your socks." When Jerry asked Rosemary later where that story came from, it was clear she had simply made it up on the spot. Still, it brought the house down.

The award recognized her "as an internationally renowned plantswoman, garden designer, and writer. Mrs. Verey's garden at Barnsley House, one of England's finest and most famous, delights thousands of visitors in practice and through the written word. Mrs. Verey's lifetime of gardening has offered boundless inspiration." The medal itself was for her "overwhelming personal and professional commitment to advancing the world-wide interest in horticulture through her writings and lectures and especially by sharing her magnificent garden at Barnsley House." The English horticultural establishment would not finally award her their highest honor until the following year.

CHAPTER ELEVEN

Garden Styles Move On
Late 1990s

I don't know what all the fuss is about.
Why, that's what I have been doing all along!

OWARDS THE END of the 1990s, Rosemary was in her late seventies, and though she pushed on in her work, her health continued to decline. She also faced a public shift in taste away from her traditional garden style. Still worse, she had a falling out with Prince Charles. Before this unexplained rift and while her treasured friendship with Prince Charles remained sufficiently solid, she enjoyed two very special events.

The first was a talk they gave together about Prince Charles's gardens at Highgrove. Initially, Rosemary planned to speak alone, as she so often did on garden topics. But because she wished to talk about Highgrove, she correctly sought his permission, never imagining that Prince Charles would want to participate in the talk himself.

In March 1995, Rosemary and Prince Charles delivered the event of the decade. They were scheduled to appear in the Purcell Room on the South Bank of London for the benefit of the National Trust. When word got out that Prince Charles would be speaking too, the sponsors had to find a larger room to accommodate the clamoring crowd and the talk was moved to Queen Elizabeth Hall. Those who attended remember the interaction of this special twosome as quite charming. Rosemary deferred to Prince Charles, but there was a give and take, back and forth, to the delight of their audience. At one point, she called him Charles in front of the audience, then quickly corrected herself to use the appropriate "Sir."

At the end of that year and no doubt in large part thanks to Prince Charles, the name Mrs. R. I. B. Verey, author and horticulturist, was included on the Queen's New Year's Honours List; she was to receive an Order of the British Empire (OBE), among the highest honors awarded by the Crown.[1] There are varying levels of Royal Orders of Chivalry, which were first established by King George V in 1917. Rosemary's client, Elton John had previously received the slightly higher level of Commander of the British Empire (CBE), then later received a knighthood which entitled him to be addressed forever after as "Sir" Elton. Rosemary was not entitled to any honorific form of address before her name, but thereafter she could proudly include the letters OBE after it.

Queen Elizabeth signed the official citation at the top; it says, "Given at our court at St. James this 30th day of December 1995 by Sovereign's Command." Prince Philip, as Grand Master, signed at the bottom "Philip." Rosemary's formal investiture took place the following year at Buckingham Palace at 11 A.M. on October 26, 1996. Prince Charles presided. She is listed under the Most Excellent Order of the British Empire in the Civil Division as "Rosemary, Mrs. Verey, for services to horticulture." For royalist Rosemary, this was a singular honor, and she was justifiably proud of it.

Her penultimate book, *Rosemary Verey's Making of a Garden*, came out in 1995. In it, she told her story of creating the Barnsley gardens. There are wonderful photographs of the gardens taken by Tony Lord, a surprising change from Rosemary's friend Andrew Lawson, who was disappointed not to have been given this assignment. The early family photographs in the book, showing Barnsley and its grounds when Rosemary was still a young wife and mother, speak volumes about the transformation she and David created. One reviewer reported that "her direct approach and honesty is refreshing. It is what the average individual wants to hear, a reassurance that if she could do something extraordinary, then the rest of us can also aspire to a degree of success."[2]

In that same year, she received the Garden Writers Guild's Lifetime Achievement Award for her outstanding contribution to the gardening media. The year before, one additional book, *Secret Gardens: Revealed by Their Owners*, was published. It was selected and edited by Rosemary Verey and Katherine Lambert, but once again, Rosemary did not write more than the introduction. The book follows the successful formula of her first books, consisting of a collection of essays written by the garden owners. There are forty-eight of them with gardens in England, France, Germany, the Netherlands, Belgium, Portugal, and Canada, with seventeen of the gardens – over a third – in America.

The introduction to *Secret Gardens* is a long, learned historical tale of secret gardens dating back to the Persians and Egyptians. There are many references to and quotes from sixteenth- and seventeenth-century books in her library. She concludes, "We must never forget the lessons from the past and new secret gardens will always be created. Today Barbara Robinson's and Oscar de la Renta's gardens, both in Connecticut, are magic oases among hills and woodland where you may pause awhile and time stands still. These gardens, and others like them, are sanctuaries for the owners as they escape from the demands and pounding bustle of modern life. I am forever making new discoveries – this is what life is all about and what makes it so exciting."[3]

Her last book was produced in conjunction with her one and only foray into the world of television. Although she had been on television for an occasional interview, she had never had a major show of her own.[4] *The English Country Garden* was published by BBC Books in 1996 to accompany the major television series, with photographs by her perennial favorites, Andrew Lawson and Jerry Harpur. The series and book featured twelve gardens, including her own Barnsley House and Elton John's Woodside along with Christopher Lloyd's Great Dixter and Winfield House, the American Ambassador's residence in Regent's Park. Almost all the gardens are rather grand affairs. In her introduction, Rosemary ties the gardens into their history, with only three having been created in recent years. She highlights Elton John's Woodside because she "wanted to include one garden I had helped to design. . . . It is never open to the public, but a glimpse in this book and on television is a chance to enjoy his taste – the first thought he passed on to me was his love of cottage garden flowers." Then she tactfully adds, "Now his horizon has widened and his garden is changing."[5]

BBC2 produced seven programs in the series. The format had Rosemary strolling through the featured garden in the company of its owner while having a friendly conversation as the cameras rolled. It must have seemed like a good idea, enlisting Rosemary's knowledge and charm in a chat while she and the owner took the audience on a walk through a spectacular garden. Some have speculated that as a reputation begins to lose luster, the fading star may take to television in the hopes of salvaging their fame. If that was the hope, it failed here.

Perhaps it was simply that the medium did not suit Rosemary's personality. Somehow her charm and vivacity did not come across on camera. Even her friends and neighbors

LEFT: *Sir Elton John and David Furnish in costume for Elton's fiftieth birthday party, 1997.*

BELOW: *The scented garden and rill at Woodside, Old Windsor.*

LEFT: *Rosemary Verey with His Royal Highness The Prince of Wales in the Cottage Garden at his home at Highgrove.*

BELOW: *A view of the Cottage Garden at Highgrove.*

ABOVE: *Rosemary Verey confers with a Japanese delegation asking her to design model gardens at Hankyu Department Store, Osaka, Japan.*

BELOW LEFT: *Rosemary Verey and the author in their Oscar de la Renta dresses at her eightieth birthday party at Tate Britain, 1998.*

BELOW RIGHT: *Rosemary Verey and Christopher Lloyd at her eightieth birthday party at Tate Britain, 1998.*

LEFT: *Rosemary Verey wearing an Irish cap at her desk in The Close.*

RIGHT: *Richard and Sheila Sanford's herbaceous borders within a yew hedge with views of the Brandywine countryside beyond.*

BELOW: *The last garden. A potager for Antony and Angela Beck, Gainesway, Lexington, Kentucky.*

found her disappointing. One observed that "she was not very good on television. She didn't come over very well."[6] Her conversations with the garden owners, most of whom were British upper class and spoke in distinctly impenetrable upper-class accents, caused her own English accent to thicken and become even more upper crust. To an American ear, at least, these accents, with the mumbled, swallowed sentence endings made most of the conversations incomprehensible. Unlike so many other BBC productions, this one never came to America, and it was not widely popular even in the United Kingdom. One newspaper reported that the series had been described in various trade publications as a "sleeper, slow but steady, it climbs in popularity. It has gently hooked me."[7] Apparently it didn't hook too many others. Rosemary never participated in another television series or program. The companion book was the last she would ever write.

If Rosemary did not prove to be a TV star, she continued to shine before audiences in her own garden. Huge numbers of visitors continued to arrive at Barnsley each year from around the world. Many came from England, Europe, and America, but busloads began to come from Japan, then emerging as among the strongest and richest economies of the world. Japanese companies were gobbling up prime English and American real estate, their acquisition of a major stake in New York's Rockefeller Center just one prominent example. They tended to travel in groups rather than separately because of the language difficulty, usually following the ubiquitous tour leader waving a Japanese flag.

Just down the road from Barnsley, the village of Bibury, with its fish hatchery and picturesque Cotswold buildings, became a favorite Japanese destination, so Barnsley comfortably fit their itinerary, and Japanese tourists began visiting

Rosemary's garden in increasing numbers. Since the Japanese have their own quite distinctive garden style, one that doesn't feature flowers and favors a spare look, it is surprising that they took such delight in Rosemary's profuse, flowery style. Perhaps as they sought to acquire the best of the West, Barnsley caught their fancy. Whatever the reason, Rosemary's garden was considered among the prime horticultural examples of England and they flocked to Barnsley.

By 1996, Rosemary had become so famous in Japan that a delegation of three Japanese gentlemen arrived to ask her to design a garden for them in Osaka. Elegantly dressed in formal suits, vests, and ties, the three men performed their obligatory bowing when they first met, then sat down together with Rosemary around her dining room table. Since this was the room where Rosemary worked, the table was covered with her customary books, correspondence, slides, and various ongoing projects. One of the gentlemen, able to speak a heavily accented English, served as the spokesman for the trio, translating as the conversation progressed.

Their mission was to persuade Rosemary to design and install a model English garden in the Hankyu Department Store located in Osaka, Japan. It was to be like the model gardens at the Chelsea Flower Show and part of a British Fair they were organizing for the following year. The British Fair was being co-sponsored by the British Embassy and British Consul. The three Japanese representatives made it clear that they wanted to have a quintessential English garden, so they had come to the person they considered the most famous designer of quintessential English gardens, Rosemary Verey. There followed a long, oblique, polite conversation throughout which Rosemary tried valiantly to say no. While Rosemary was flattered to be asked, she insisted that she was not up to going herself, given the difficulties of the distance and the length of the trip. The delegation continued to press, assuring her that they most wanted her design even if they couldn't count on her presence.

Ever practical, Rosemary suggested that it would be extremely difficult for her to source the proper plants, never mind oversee the installation from so far away. The logistics seemed impossible for anyone, even someone half her age. (She was then seventy-eight.) But at the end of this delicate dance, she yielded, and as usual she enlisted a coterie of talented friends and helpers.

Paul Miles, a professional designer himself and a friend since the 1960s from their shared participation in the Garden Historical Society, took on the principal responsibility for making the garden happen. Paul remembered staying with Rosemary a few years after David's death and saying, "I am going to propose to you this evening. If you do not accept my proposal, I shall jump off a bridge!" Taking this in, Rosemary "took off her spectacles, polished them, then looked at me with a gleam and said, 'Tell me which bridge!'" Paul was the perfect partner in this ambitious undertaking and knew how to work well with Rosemary.

Andrew Lawson was also enlisted. He agreed to deliver a few talks about Rosemary's gardens, illustrated by his magnificent slides of Barnsley. The Japanese were particularly interested in Rosemary's famous potager, but Andrew would also bring pictures of other gardens Rosemary had worked on, including a knot garden for the Misses Barrie's house at Broadway, the Elizabethan Garden at Holdenby House for the Lowthers, and the Reynolds' Little House apple tunnel in full bloom. Charles Verey committed to go as well to promote his teak garden furniture and explore commercial possibilities of licensing Rosemary's name. Her book, *A Countrywoman's Notes*, was translated into Japanese and sold at the Hankyu show.

There were four different garden areas designed by Rosemary: a container garden, an herb garden, a fragrant garden, and a rose garden. Rosemary sent her favorite quotation from John Evelyn that had been inscribed on her own plinth at the end of the laburnum walk to be used on a sundial for the gardens, "As no man be very miserable that is master of a Garden here; so will no man ever be happy who is not sure of a Garden hereafter. . . . Where the first Adam fell, the second rose." And although she couldn't appear in person, she sent a personal touch. Her hat and trug were placed prominently on the bench in the rose garden.

The preparatory work began shortly after this delegation had visited Barnsley; the British Fair opened the following year of 1997 on the sixth floor of Osaka's Hankyu Department Store. Much larger than the famous Harrods of London, Hankyu had grown after the Second World War by building a chain of department stores over train stations throughout Japan. In a display of Japanese efficiency, Rosemary's gardens, along with a full theater and a large sales area, were fully installed in a single day.

The ceremonies opened with great fanfare. The formalities began with a group of Japanese dignitaries standing in a long line, each dressed in a formal dark suit adorned with a single red carnation in his lapel. They faced a line of their counterparts from England. On precise signal, there were formal bows followed by the two lines walking past each other, shaking hands as they went by, looking slightly like a formal dress version of two hockey teams skating past each other shaking gloves after a game. Andrew Lawson was called upon to read a special letter of greeting from Prince Charles as part of the opening ceremonies. With the formalities over, the doors opened to the waiting crowds.

It was almost as if Rosemary had become the Laura Ashley of gardening. The theater was the venue for a schedule of lectures. Paul Miles not only supervised the garden installation, he and Andrew Lawson both delivered several talks. The sales of small gardening goods and other British products exceeded all expectations. It was a triumph.

But as the Japanese were celebrating the Rosemary Verey style, her star was beginning to wane in other quarters. New designers were seizing the stage. Designers such as James van Sweden and Wolfgang Oehme and Piet Oudolf were appearing on the scene, with the "New Wave" or "New Perennial" style of planting. The so-called Dutch or German movement espoused "natural" planting in large drifts, particularly emphasizing the use of swaths of ornamental grasses. Plants formerly considered weeds were the "new perennials," to be planted in natural, ecologically balanced communities. In America, it would be called prairie style; in England, meadows would become the vogue. There was little emphasis on color or interest in constant bloom; rather than formal structures, the focus was to be on the structures of the plants themselves, especially on dying fall foliage left standing through the winter. While Rosemary's book *The Garden in Winter* had been groundbreaking, its view of a garden in winter spoke of evergreens, berries, and branch structures, not necessarily the stems and leaves of dead plants.

English gardening was beginning to move in a very different direction toward this naturalistic look with ornamental grasses, and Rosemary knew it. In 1994, she attended a symposium at Kew dominated by the Dutch-German speakers talking about this new style of planting. The program was organized by her friends Stephen Lacey and Tim Rees, along with Brita von Schoenaich. While the English approach was "out of chaos comes order," Tim Rees saw the German approach as being the opposite, "out of order comes chaos." At first glance, the resulting naturalistic look seemed quite artless, but it reflected the German penchant for precision. To achieve the effect, a master plan for the plantings had to be strictly adhered to.

Rosemary's English country house formal style had become so prevalent and she was so widely known that this "New Wave" was a direct reaction against her. She was the embodiment of a particular flowery style. So it surprised Tim Rees to hear her reaction after the symposium was over. She said very simply, "I don't know what all the fuss is about. Why, that's what I have been doing all along!"

Rosemary's statement at first blush seemed ridiculous. However, Tim believes that Rosemary meant that her thickly planted borders, while tightly constrained within formal lines, were allowed to rip. Her plantings were exuberant, the plants allowed to interweave and grow through one another in the same spirit of this natural garden style, although certainly not with the same look. And she certainly allowed many plants to self-seed and certain seed heads to remain standing for winter interest. But Tim observed that "hers was born of experience and intuition." Rather than sticking to a master plan, Rosemary was "much more organic and allowed things to evolve." Tim called hers "naturalized borders, much more Robinsonian." Her approach had plants grouped for color and tone, rather than ecological principles. While Rosemary certainly knew what conditions particular plants required to thrive, she didn't talk the language of ecology. She just practiced it. And she never really adopted grasses. The color orange was not to be seen in her garden. Hers were flower borders, in soft pastels and presenting a very different palette of plants.

Not all venues continued to clamor for her to come and speak. She was "sort of over-exposed. Everybody had heard her plenty," Gregory Long recalled. It was a major blow when her reliable Bailey brothers quit, after having worked as her main gardeners for fifteen years. Together, they had been a reliable threesome, part of "the golden age when the garden was in its prime."[8] With their departure and her declining health, Rosemary was fortunate to hire Nick Burton as her head gardener, although like others before him, Nick quickly learned that "there was only one head gardener" and that was Rosemary. Although it was very much her garden still, he did relieve her of some of the pressure of its upkeep.

Nick absorbed a great many of Rosemary's rules, especially her insistent refrain, "Use your eyes, Nick, use your eyes!" She herself was always looking, spotting things that could be improved or removed. And if a job "needs doing, do it properly. If you can do it once instead of twice, do it once." Every day started with the dead heading to make everything look perfect. Nick learned how much you "could grow in a relatively small space, with the layering of plants," and an emphasis on the corners. "The corners had to look good because that's where the eye went first."

Like other gardeners before him, Nick also learned when to keep his head down. Whenever they heard her study door rattle, it was the signal. The gardeners heard that and said, "Right. Buck-up. She's out." Nick lived on "his nerves working for her" and knew each day depended upon how much she had to drink. The more she had to drink the more unpredictable and volatile she became. And the more pain she endured, the more she needed to drink.

Once when a visitor mistook Nick for Rosemary's husband, Nick told Rosemary about it. Her quick retort was, "I am not into toy boys yet." He also remembers conspiratorially hiding from garden visitors. Once when a horde of Japanese arrived, the two of them tried to hide, "crawling behind plants so we wouldn't be spotted and then ending up giggling. She could be a bit naughty sometimes." But usually "she liked meeting the people who came and they certainly liked meeting her."

One day when Nick found Rosemary upset and in tears, he tried to comfort her as best he could. That was a mistake. Rosemary resisted revealing her vulnerable side to anyone and after that episode, things changed. "There are lines" – lines not to be crossed.

Characteristically, Rosemary never spoke to anyone about a development that troubled her profoundly. Something had caused a rift between Rosemary and Prince Charles. Whether Prince Charles merely wanted to move on to newer designers or something else happened is impossible to know. Rosemary never spoke of the cause to others, so the reasons are conjectural. But friends and reporters have speculated as to what caused the break.

One friend believes that Rosemary wrote an angry letter to Prince Charles complaining that he had not asked her to help him write his first book about Highgrove as she thought he had promised. This first book was written in 1993 with co-author Charles Clover, and it seems true that Prince Charles did not ask for Rosemary's help, nor did he mention her contribution to Highgrove very much at all. Instead, the book emphasized his growing interest in organic gardening methods and gave great credit to Lady Salisbury and Miriam Rothschild for their roles in helping him develop Highgrove.[9] Some friends have speculated that Rosemary was sufficiently upset that while in her cups she sent an insulting letter to Prince Charles. That seems unlikely, since just a few years after this book was published, Prince Charles was arranging to appear on stage with Rosemary to deliver their joint lecture about Highgrove.

It is true that Rosemary participated in correspondence about a possible later book for Prince Charles in 1996. Through his office, she drafted many letters to prominent people, some of whom had played a role in the development of the gardens at Highgrove, asking them to contribute an individual chapter. Andrew Lawson was to take the pictures. This would have followed her favorite format of collecting essays written by others. Nothing came of her efforts.

Others believe Rosemary tried to prevent Prince Charles from firing the head gardener, David Magson, her principal ally at Highgrove. Rosemary and David Magson had worked closely and well together. In her usual generous way, Rosemary helped Magson find another position after he left Highgrove.[10] Her relationship with David Howard, the successor head gardener, was polite at best but never close.

Whatever the cause, the Prince's protective staff began to keep the Prince insulated from Rosemary in contrast to her previously easy and direct access to him. The estrangement was visible enough to be noted by the press, with the *Saturday Times*, reporting that a rift had occurred, "a feature of many of Verey's working relationships,"[11] suggesting that she was angry not to be consulted about Highgrove's show garden for the Chelsea Flower Show in 1998.

Just like her relationship with the Prince, even her Cottage Garden at Highgrove began to decline. It had always been in a difficult spot, and Rosemary had designed it primarily for spring interest because the Prince and his family were off to Scotland at the end of each summer. The Cottage

Garden only "had to look good when he (Prince Charles) was there. He used to go up to Scotland in August so it only had to look good up to the end of July, but then the visitors started so the garden had to look good for a much longer period of time. Certainly in the last years that she was alive, I remember her being very upset because she wanted to redo it, to change it, with the new parameters, but David Howard, the head gardener, was very – well his interpersonal skills are not always very good." And she was being shut out. "She was very hurt because she would write letters and he would never respond and she was never sure if the Prince of Wales got hers, so she was really quite hurt about that," remembers Marguerite Hoffnung, who had worked for Rosemary and became one of the first Highgrove garden guides.

James Aldridge, who worked at Highgrove, observed that when David Howard took charge as head gardener, the entire Cottage Garden border was replanted without strict adherence to Rosemary's original design. In a very short period of time, fewer than half of her original plants survived. Things had changed. Perhaps her style of planting in complicated layers was not to David Howard's taste. It certainly took great skill and intense work to keep her border looking its best, requiring close attention to cutting things back, ripping plants out, dividing others and inserting fresh plants in the gaps as the season progressed.

Her close friend Carolyn North, like Marguerite, became one of the first garden guides at Highgrove, thanks to Rosemary. Carolyn had grown up with Rosemary's children and returned to live in a nearby village after her own husband died, becoming a regular helper at Barnsley. In some ways, she almost became a substitute daughter for Rosemary in her last years, but the relationship was less complex and challenging than Rosemary's relationship with her own daughters. In return, Rosemary recommended Carolyn as one of the first garden guides at Highgrove when it became increasingly open to public visitors. After Carolyn received a call from Highgrove, she immediately called Rosemary, demanding "What have you done now Rosemary?!" She felt much too shy and not quite up to it, but Rosemary retorted, "You've got to do it, it's good for you." So Carolyn did.

Carolyn confirms that there was a cooling off period with Prince Charles, but she never knew the reason why. She believes Rosemary really loved Prince Charles and saw him as a much misunderstood, very good-hearted person. During this period of estrangement, Rosemary rather brazenly asked Carolyn to take her to the Highgrove Christmas party since each garden guide was invited and allowed to bring one additional guest. Naturally, Prince Charles was surprised to see Rosemary at this event and greeted her by saying, "What are you doing here, Rosemary? You can come here any time you like," implying she did not have to come as a guest of a guide, but continued to be welcome.

Despite the change in garden taste, her personal disappointments, and increasing frailty, Rosemary refused to give in. Even though two cataract operations in January of 1998 took a toll, leaving her feeling unsteady, she continued to push herself, traveling to the United States several times each year. She worked on designs and consulted with many private gardeners there, almost to the exclusion of work in England and the continent. By the end of 1998, Rosemary would turn eighty, an event that inspired a series of extraordinary celebrations in Gloucestershire and London. Best of all, her impending birthday celebrations resulted in a rapprochement with Prince Charles.

CHAPTER TWELVE

The Last Few Years
1998–2000

It's a sin to be dull.

OSEMARY'S EIGHTIETH birthday inspired a series of gala celebrations. Her family and many friends organized several parties that extended over a period of the weeks around December 21, 1998. Rosemary always loved a good party and, even more, loved to be the center of attention. At all of these fetes, she was the star attraction. But perhaps the best birthday present of all was her public reconciliation with Prince Charles.

First there was an intimate party for her extended family where poignantly Rosemary was now one of only two surviving members of her generation, the other being Gillian Lady Sandilands, her childhood friend and the widow of Rosemary's favorite brother, Francis. While the children also attended some of the other celebrations, this party was their own, a time to toast their mother in the arms of her family.

Oddly enough, there was no major event in the United States, even though Rosemary spent many of her happiest times there and had a vast network of friends. But she was showered with cards, messages, and gifts sent by her many American admirers, as well as from fans at home in England and other countries around the globe.

The most newsworthy party was the one hosted by her Gloucestershire friends, Anne and Vic Norman, who tried valiantly to keep their arrangements a surprise, especially about the role of Prince Charles. But the more they tried to conceal their plans, the harder Rosemary tried to wheedle and pry the truth out of them and their various co-conspirators. Rosemary fought with Carolyn North, one of the conspirators, about this for weeks. She insisted on knowing who had been invited, but Carolyn wouldn't tell. "She was really horrible to me. Totally relentless." Carolyn finally yielded and told her most of it beforehand, excepting the biggest surprise.

Victor Norman, a licensed pilot and stuntman, kept a small airplane in a hangar on his property. For Rosemary's eightieth-birthday party, the Normans decked this hangar out with charming decorations that transformed it into a potting shed. At the center of each table there was a pot of herbs, with a rosemary plant in the center. The hangar had plenty of room for a large crowd. These guests were a lovely mix of local neighbors, fellow parishioners from her church, and friends, along with many whose names are famous in horticultural circles.

Victor Norman had planned to fly over to Barnsley to pick up Rosemary but the weather was too foul. Instead, he took her up for a ride in his plane from the landing field on his property and flew her around the airfield a few times. This was the scene of the famous loop-de-loop story, and when they landed, Rosemary climbed out of the plane to meet the Prince of Wales smiling broadly and reaching his arms out to greet her. That he was indeed there, having come to honor her, was the best way to publicly announce that they were good friends again.

Another celebratory private dinner was organized by her American friend, neighbor, and garden design client, Arthur Reynolds, along with Sir Roy Strong at the Garrick Club in London. The last party was a black tie affair hosted by Rosemary's late husband's cousin, David Verey, at the Tate Gallery.

A prominent banker, then head of Lazard Frères in London and Chairman of the Board of Trustees of the Tate Gallery (now Tate Britain), David Verey arranged to open the museum for this private party for Rosemary. At the time, the Tate was featuring a magnificent exhibit of paintings by John Singer Sargent that was attracting huge crowds. It seemed somehow fitting that the exhibit should feature an American painter.

The *beau monde* of the horticultural world came, along with Rosemary's special friends and all of her children. Entering the handsome, imposing, classical building of the Tate Gallery for the evening's gala, with the banks of the River Thames beyond, was an extraordinary experience. Once inside, the guests enjoyed cocktails while strolling through the magnificent Sargent exhibition before being ushered into the formal dinner in the Trustees' Dining Room, where the walls were covered by beautiful murals. Among the many horticultural greats present were Christopher Lloyd, Penelope Hobhouse, Robin Lane Fox (garden writer for the *Financial Times*), and many more. There were eloquent toasts followed by enthusiastic applause. Rosemary was radiant in her brightly colored dress, a gift of Oscar de la Renta.

While plans were underway for these wonderful parties, an American writer, Paula Deitz, happened to be hard at work on an article that appeared in the *New York Times* on July 16, 1998, entitled "Free to Grow Bluebells in England." This told the true story about a group of prisoners in a low-security prison, Leyhill, located in the Cotswolds. The prisoners had just won a gold medal for the model garden they had designed and installed at the Hampton Court Palace Flower Show. By pure happenstance, a filmmaker walking his dog in New York City that night, stood catching up on that day's newspaper reading by the light of a street lamp. He found the story intriguing, and over the next year, he helped produce a delightful film entitled *Greenfingers* about these gardening prisoners, but with the addition of a fictional Rosemary-like patroness named Georgina Woodhouse. The film was to star Helen Mirren in this role, and part of the film featuring the fictional Georgina Woodhouse was filmed at Barnsley.

In her words, Mirren "very much wanted to meet a character that was as close to the character I was playing as possible. The horticultural world is not one I'm hugely familiar with and it's very much a world unto itself, with its own hierarchy and its own characters." As a result, a visit was arranged, and Helen Mirren was introduced to Rosemary. Insisting that she did not base her character entirely on Rosemary, Helen Mirren acknowledges that Rosemary was the only person she met before deciding how to play this role. Having only dallied in a bit of home gardening before this encounter, Ms. Mirren was fascinated to learn more about the complicated world of horticulture.

Even at Rosemary's advanced age, Helen Mirren found her to be "about the most intimidating person I'd ever met." At their first meeting she found her "abrupt in style, until she warmed to you. It wasn't like the movie star meeting the gardener. It was the star gardener meeting some foreign little actress." Until Rosemary did warm up, the actress found her "really quite spiky."

By virtue of her profession and her talent as an actress, Ms. Mirren is a keen observer of character; she saw Rosemary as a "grand egotist. But people who are very good at their craft or their art or their profession are like that. You have to be a grand egotist. Like a conductor, a great artist. And I would say Rosemary fitted into that category from my perception, that sense of autocracy, self-confidence, leadership, but enormous self confidence," at least in her work. And a sense of "it will be done my way or it won't be done." She saw Rosemary as "someone who wouldn't suffer fools gladly. You had to prove yourself. She wasn't going to make it easy for you."[1]

Over the course of their three-hour visit, Rosemary did warm up considerably and eventually evinced some of the famous Rosemary Verey charm. Helen ended up liking her a lot, and she thought her garden was absolutely beautiful. As they walked around Barnsley, Rosemary was very keen for Helen Mirren to appreciate her as "a hands-on gardener, perfectly capable of getting down on her hands and knees and digging a hole or weeding herself or putting in the right earth." Seeing the garden firsthand, Mirren began to grasp what it was all about and she certainly was able to "appreciate what an honor it was."

Helen Mirren claimed she wasn't playing Rosemary in the character of Georgina Woodhouse, writing to Rosemary afterward, "For myself, the time I spent with you was invaluable. For while I hasten to say that the character I play is nothing like you at all, I learnt a lot about what kind of energy, commitment, dedication, and good old-fashioned very hard work it takes to create the kind of garden you have made. I shall remember Barnsley and your blue eyes always."[2] Notwithstanding her contention, Rosemary seems very much in evidence in the film.

The British horticultural establishment took a long time before recognizing Rosemary. It was not until 1999 that Rosemary received the highest honor awarded by the Royal Horticultural Society, its Victoria Medal of Honour. Many thought it long overdue. The Royal Horticultural Society is the ultimate establishment of British gardening. Begun in 1804 with the Queen as its patron, it is the leading garden charity in England. Among many programs, it runs the famous Chelsea Flower Show each year, as well as many other smaller flower shows around the country and more recently the Hampton Court Palace event featured in Helen Mirren's film, *Greenfingers*. It has an extraordinary library and owns and operates major public gardens throughout the United Kingdom, including Wisley, Harlow Carr, Hyde Hall, and Rosemoor. Yet Rosemary had never been invited to serve on the RHS Board or on its Councils.[3] Nor had she ever been asked to design any part of its many public gardens. By contrast, Lady Salisbury serves as a Vice President and Penelope Hobhouse was commissioned to design a garden at Wisley.

The medal was established in 1897 to commemorate the sixty-three years of Queen Victoria's reign. Symbolically, there can only be sixty-three living medal holders at any one time. Until a medal holder dies, no new one can be awarded. Therefore, there are years when no medals can be bestowed and other years in which multiple medals are granted. Rosemary was nearing the end of her life when she received hers. The Victoria Medal of Honour sat proudly displayed in its original case on Rosemary's fireplace mantel in her dining room/study until she died.

Despite her poor health, she continued to travel to the United States. In September of 1999, she went to deliver five different lectures for the Royal Oak Foundation, the American affiliate of the British National Trust. At one point during this trip, she noted in her diary she had painful shingles, a high temperature, and a loss of muscle strength. Only to her diary did she confide that "some days I have a hard time getting out of the borders. My legs won't help me and going up and down steps is hard. By P.M. I'm often hopeless. Doctor says it's P.M.R. or muscle rheumatism." She was taking three steroids a day for strength and to recover from an infection. But she got "full attention at JFK. Wheel chair waiting, straight through customs and there was [some friend's] limo waiting."[4] Notwithstanding her condition, on a single day, she went to the New York Botanical Garden to work on her potager design there, fit in a dinner with Oscar de la Renta, and after dinner returned to her room where she signed three boxes of her book *The English Country Garden* and reviewed her NYBG plans for meetings the following day.

Renny Reynolds, the famous American floral designer-arranger and adorner of the most fabulous parties, and his partner, Jack Staub, were part of the Royal Oak group who invited her to speak. Renny remembers that "the spirit was definitely there . . . but she was not at the top of her game. . . . She was very frail and quite honestly it was not a great lecture. The energy that I had seen the year before had waned, yet she was sharing ideas and knowledge, and she stood up and did it. Her voice was kind of failing, but she stood up and did it."

Only eleven days later, she was off again in mid October, flying to Charleston, South Carolina, for the Garden Conservancy's tenth anniversary celebration. Despite difficulty walking, she resisted all offers of assistance, attended all the talks, and got herself on and off the busses to visit historic gardens in the area with the rest of the crowd. She even managed to get out on the dance floor with a chivalrous man, who held her standing in his arms without moving his feet, the two of them gently swaying to the music of Lester Lanin.

Toward the end of 1999 Rosemary fell and broke her hip, an injury exacerbated by the break she had suffered on that same side when she broke her femur in a riding accident as a much younger woman. That earlier break complicated the process for dealing with this blow. At first, the doctors tried a method less intrusive than a complete hip replacement, putting in a pin to try to hold the hip together. After a lengthy recovery, the operation was considered a failure. The entire procedure had to be completely re-done. Enduring a second operation in relatively short succession left Rosemary very weak and never fully able to walk strongly again.

She soldiered on, pushing herself as hard as she could. And she continued to travel to America. After another fall that left half her face black and blue, she insisted on going to New York for a Garden Conservancy tour of Long Island gardens, even though she could barely walk. But she was beginning to realize she could not manage everything as she had before. During that year, she was asked to participate in a design competition for the walled garden at Osborne House on the Isle of Wight, the former summer residence of Queen Victoria and Prince Albert. The competition, sponsored by English Heritage (which owned this historic property and opened it to the public) was part of its Contemporary English Garden Initiative intended to create new contemporary gardens within historic settings. Five designers were chosen to submit their plans for this one-acre area within walls that had once sheltered the kitchen garden at Osborne House. Rosemary was among those invited, and among the others was her one-time gardener and protégé, Rupert Golby.

Deborah Goodenough was then the head gardener there, responsible for the restoration of all the Osborne House gardens. She remembers Rosemary coming to look at the site early that year. As they walked around, Rosemary chatted with Deborah and was charming. Although it is doubtful that Rosemary remembered her, Deborah had been to Barnsley a decade before as a young student at Kew. She bumped into

Rosemary in the garden when Rosemary must have been having a bad moment. This time, they got along very well, but ultimately Rosemary decided to withdraw, realizing it was too much for her.

Each of the other competitors went to the site independently and they weren't supposed to swap ideas. After she withdrew, she called Rupert Golby and offered to give him all her notes. Rupert found this quite tricky when Rosemary suggested this could be a combined effort because Rupert had independent ideas of his own. Nevertheless, it was hard to refuse her, so Rupert did borrow all the books she offered him and listened to her suggestions. In due course, Rupert was chosen. At first he didn't tell Rosemary but made a date to return all her books. He arrived with the books and said, "There's a bottle of champagne there too." When she asked why, he told her "I won it and I'm going to do it. And she couldn't have been more pleased. She said, 'If I had won it, I wouldn't have been half as pleased as if you'd won it.'" Always generous in her support and promotion of her garden protégés, her pleasure was genuine.

When her friend from Dallas, Carl Neels, heard she had broken her hip, he expected to cancel his scheduled Thanksgiving holiday visit, but Rosemary's daughter Veronica called to tell him Rosemary wanted him to come stay at her house even though she was in the Cheltenham General Hospital. He complied and went to visit her at the hospital. He shouldn't have been surprised that Rosemary managed to get her own way even in hospital. She said to him, "I'm getting kind of thirsty. Would you like something to drink?" When he agreed, she summoned the nurse and said, "Would you please bring us two gin and tonics?" Carl thought she must have been mistaken until the nurse returned, carrying their drinks!

Finally, Rosemary decided it was time to put her son Charles in charge of the management of the garden. But Charles was an inexperienced gardener, and Rosemary had spent her life being in command. It was a delicate dance. That December, Charles decided to hire Richard Gatenby as head gardener. And although he was nominally called the "head gardener," he quickly realized, like many before him, that "there was only one head gardener" at Barnsley, and that was still Rosemary, even if she had officially delegated the garden to Charles and through him to Richard. While her intellect told her she had to let go, the garden had been the core of her life for too many years. Charles Verey tried his best.

Richard was often caught in between. Whenever Charles went away, Richard knew that Rosemary would be on him, telling Richard what to do. Once when Charles was away on a long trip to Turkey, she commanded Richard to do something she wanted done, but Charles had left other instructions. Charles had asked Richard to put up a new poly tunnel, a very big job, and have it finished before he returned. Rosemary confronted Richard and asked him, "Are you going to do what I'm telling you to do?" Finally Richard had to tell her the truth and replied, "No, Mrs. Verey. Charles asked me to do this and he wants it done." Rosemary was furious. Richard saw her grip the handle of the Aga in her kitchen so fiercely he thought she would tear it off. However, by the next day, they were friends again.

Barnsley was a wonderful place for Richard to work and learn from Rosemary even though Charles was formally in charge. He knew she was a disciplinarian and forthright, that if she asked you to do something, "She wanted it done right then and there. You wouldn't dare to think that you would do it in an hour's time." And although the garden was enormously labor-intensive, Rosemary told him, "We don't do things because they're labor-saving or low-maintenance or because they're horticulturally correct. We do them because they're pretty." While she was "a control freak," she wasn't a control freak in the garden, because she let it be, like riding a horse. "You don't pull it to bits with the reins, you let it run, and she was a brilliant rider. So she was very soft with the garden."

Toward the end of her life, Rosemary began to entertain thoughts of preserving Barnsley after her death. Even though she had given the ownership of Barnsley to Charles in 1987, she confided in her friend Anne Norman that she wanted to take it back.[5] In reviewing her estate plan and consulting her independent advisers, she considered various options, outlining four of them for herself: Charles could continue to own Barnsley with Rosemary still living there as things stood; she could take Barnsley back and rent it out; she could form a corporation to own it for the benefit of all four children; or she could create a foundation to buy the property and preserve it. She even listed possible donors who might support the foundation and contribute as much as £10,000 to help perpetuate the garden. Many Americans were on her wish list, including sponsorship by the New York Botanical Garden with the help of Gregory Long, Frank Cabot, and others.[6] If the foundation idea were to succeed, she had to consider the resulting problem of where Charles and his wife Denzil would live and work.

It was too late. While the advice she received from her solicitors and tax people remains entirely confidential and private, it does not appear that she ever went any further in trying to retract her gift of Barnsley to Charles. Donors were not approached and other than her personal notes and her remarks to Anne Norman, who told her she couldn't undo what she had already done, Rosemary did not discuss this with others. By 1999, she no longer allowed herself the luxury of second thoughts. Barnsley's future was entirely in the hands of Charles.

CHAPTER THIRTEEN

The Final Garden
2001

I hope to create a garden which feels loved
and longs to be walked in.[1]

VEN THOUGH she could barely walk, Rosemary tried to resume her public life after her hip healed enough to allow her to move around, although she did so with difficulty. She was not an easy patient (she liked to be in charge) and she was not good at accepting help offered by others. The role didn't suit her. She must have been in pain for most of the last years of her life even though she didn't complain. And chronic pain may well have caused her eruptions of bad temper.

In 2000, The National Portrait Gallery mounted the exhibition *Five Centuries of Women and Gardens*, with a companion book written by Sue Bennett. Rosemary was prominently included. The exhibit featured the likes of Gertrude Jekyll, Ellen Willmott, and Norah Lindsay; in the section on the twentieth century to the present, Rosemary was among Vita Sackville-West, Valerie Finnis, Margery Fish, and Miriam Rothschild. In the description of her work, her style was described as "informal within a formal framework."[2] Her articles for many magazines were mentioned, and her first book, *The Englishwoman's Garden*, was called "a classic of its type." Both Prince Charles at Highgrove and Elton John were noted as among her famous clients, but her potager was particularly highlighted. "Inspired by her box-edged plots of ornamental lettuces, pink and yellow cabbages, ruby chard, arbours of vines and runner beans, many other gardeners have followed her example." Then the write up concludes, "She lectures frequently in the USA."

For her portrait, there was a wonderful Howard Sooley photograph of her standing in a pale blue dress that enhanced her blue eyes. She wore her signature multi-stranded pearls and was smiling, shorn of her eyeglasses, framed by the hanging yellow blossoms of her iconic laburnum walk with the pale lavender alliums blooming underneath.

That Christmas of 2000 she planned to fly to Dallas, Texas, to celebrate the holidays with her good friend, Carl Neels. Rosemary had discovered that by asking for a wheelchair to navigate the airports, air travel was possible; she could avoid the crush of the crowds and be taken straight on and off the plane without too much strain. Even when she was in reasonably good health and didn't really need a wheelchair, she had discovered how handy it could be in her travels. Just a few years before when she flew to visit Carl for the holidays, he was surprised to see her come out in a wheelchair. As they got to his car and before he had a chance to ask why, she said, "I learned long ago if you want to get through customs without a hitch you request a wheelchair on arrival." Under her coat, she had concealed the Christmas pudding she brought for Carl.

She had also begun to work on plans for her next book, which was to be about people who had been an influence on her and helped her in her life. Many names on her list were Americans. After she announced her plan to spend Christmas in Texas to her children, they in turn made plans to be away too.

But just before that Christmas, she was stricken with

pneumonia. Even Rosemary had to concede she could not fly to Texas. Instead, the devoted Carl came to Barnsley to take care of her and make Christmas dinner for her at The Close. Carl had been at Barnsley to stay with Rosemary only a few months before in October when they planned to go to London for a few days. Just before they were about to leave, Rosemary failed to come out from behind the closed dining room doors. Because she could no longer climb the stairs to her lovely bedroom on the second floor, the dining room had been converted into her downstairs bedroom. When Carl went to knock on the door, he heard Rosemary saying to herself, "Oh please let me get up, please let me get up." When he opened the door, she was lying on the floor where she had fallen out of bed. Carl was sure their London trip had to be cancelled but Rosemary pleaded with him to just let her sleep for twenty minutes to recover. While Carl packed her bag, she napped, woke up, then got in the car for the two-hour drive to London. She managed to go out with Carl to the theater that night to see *Mamma Mia!* Clearly, she was pushing herself.

After Christmas, Carl left to return to Dallas and Paul Miles came to see in the New Year with Rosemary. He could tell she was in pain, especially in her hip and leg. Paul helped her get ready for bed in the evenings and kept her company before he headed upstairs to sleep. One night, he discovered she had managed to find a dog leash. "She would lasso her foot to get herself out of bed so she could go to the bathroom and then get herself back again. She was plucky. She was determined that if she had to get up in the night she would manage that herself."

Friends and admirers continued to arrive to see the garden but many came just to see her. Her daughter Davina became a loyal and patient caregiver, along with the help of hired professionals. Although Rosemary wasn't strong enough to go out for lunch at the local pub across the street, she continued to invite visitors to lunch with her at The Close, happy to have their company. She always put her best self forward, forcing herself out of bed, dressing carefully, and arranging her hair before summoning the energy to be her most charming, lively self. She often insisted on going out to the kitchen to see to things, bossing Davina around relentlessly.

When her grandson Robert was to be married, Rosemary refused to miss the wedding. Always careful about her appearance, she ordered a custom-made hat from the best milliner on Jermyn Street in London. It was a beautiful, large-brimmed navy affair and she looked stunning. One visitor was instructed to go upstairs to her closet and return with the hat so Rosemary could model it for her.[3]

One of Robert's American friends came soon after the wedding and asked to meet his famous grandmother. Always ready for visitors, especially a handsome young man, Rosemary met Antony Beck from Lexington, Kentucky. Although South African by birth, Antony and his family had spent some time living in the Cotswolds quite near to Barnsley. His parents had kept a horse farm there so Antony knew the area and was aware of Rosemary's garden. In the course of their conversation, Antony, in his quiet way, somehow managed to entice Rosemary into coming to Kentucky to design a garden for him. When she agreed, she explained that she would have to bring Davina as a companion in order to see the site.

In March of 2001, very much in pain and barely able to stand, Rosemary traveled first class to Kentucky accompanied by Davina. Antony and his wife, Angela Beck, met them at the airport and drove them to Gainesway, a world-class stud farm in the rolling hills and white fence country of Kentucky. Its 1500 acres had once belonged to Cornelius Vanderbilt Whitney and had bred some of the great stallions of horse racing. The Becks built a handsome Georgian-style brick house on a high spot, overlooking the spectacular view that spread out to the far horizon. Prize-winning horses grazed in the lush green fields, punctuated by clumps of trees.

Antony was captivated by Rosemary's charm and eager for her ideas. He had "expected her to arrive with a plan, but she came in and said 'What do you want, what should we do?' That's why it was five days." She spent several days sitting on Antony's terrace overlooking the grounds where his gardens were to be, down a slope toward the open fields beyond. With papers spread out on a table and blowing in the wind, Rosemary sat like a maestro conductor, pointing and directing Antony's patient gardener. As a trained landscape architect, the gardener probably had to bite his tongue as she dictated from on high, commanding him to lay out sticks and strings to mark her evolving design. But as she sat, "she got a bit exasperated," frustrated no doubt by her inability to get out of her chair and work in her usual style, laying out the shapes herself right there upon the ground. Her vantage point did give her a beautiful view of the yearlings as they were paraded in the fields beyond. Antony remembers, "There was one big chestnut filly that she really liked. I ended up keeping it, partly because she liked it."

Eventually, Antony and Rosemary decided to base the design on a walled garden at Ascott Place in Berkshire, just outside of London, that she had included in her book *Rosemary Verey's Good Planting Plans*. Although she doesn't identify the owner, Antony rightly understood it had been designed for King Hussein, and Antony loved it. Rosemary acknowledged about this plan in her book that "sadly after I had dreamed up this 'paradise' garden, the estate was sold. My plans are still only in the mind, in rough outline. It would be such a delight to carry out the detailed planting."[4]

Rosemary got her wish to implement her basic ideas in a walled potager for the Becks. Antony had already identified the area for this garden and had ordered a greenhouse for it that Rosemary helped to site. While Antony didn't think her design was particularly special, "there was certainly something special about her. But not about the design. It was geometric pleasing shapes but she had some wonderful contributions." And even though he knew she was in "her twilight, [he] remembers her as tremendously strong."

This potager is walled on most sides, with one side outlined by a hedge. Antony's charming greenhouse sits in the center of one side, its position blessed by Rosemary. She suggested that the small pool in front of the greenhouse be raised and surrounded by a low wall topped with flat stones to allow someone to stop and sit there. This is a lovely touch that seems just right. Narrow brick paths outline geometrically shaped beds in classic Rosemary style. She had thoughts about the ironwork for metal arches that Antony ordered made to her specifications in England, views on the plantings and suggestions that he has followed. Antony "truly feels her presence there very much." A beautiful potager is the result of Rosemary's work for the Becks and Antony's great love for his garden.

How appropriate that this beautiful surviving garden should contain a classic Rosemary Verey potager and that it should be in America. As she intended, it is adorned with flowers as well as vegetables and made personal by Antony. Rosemary very much wanted to return to "carry out the detailed planting" plans and develop the plant lists, as she had done with such precision with her design for a proposed potager at the New York Botanical Garden. For this once passionate horsewoman, it was especially lovely to have this garden surrounded by horses she had loved.

When Rosemary returned to Barnsley and told Gregory Long by telephone that she had been to Kentucky to design a garden, he was sure she was hallucinating. "She was so fragile, so frail, she had been in so much pain, she had so many problems, she had all of a sudden gotten on an airplane and gone to the States. I thought she was imagining it and I was humoring her. And it turned out that it was true! She had actually done that." He found it hard to believe. Two months later, on May 31, 2001, she was gone.

There was an outpouring of testimonials and eloquent obituaries in the major press. Even *The Economist*, a publication not normally given to covering horticultural news, devoted a full page to her, noting she had been an important English ambassador, especially to America. "Many Americans set their hearts on a Verey garden. It had the kind of cachet attached to, say, Harrods . . . or a Rolls-Royce."[5] Her work for Prince Charles was highlighted, as well as her "seventeen books, some of them now classics. Lecture tours followed. Potential clients lined up." She was described as part of the tradition of gifted women gardeners that went back to the sixteenth century. But *The Economist* went on to say that even in the "calming world of gardening there is what might be called landscape politics." The article suggested Rosemary's style was being eclipsed by the rise of minimalist gardens, intended to reflect modern architecture in its simplicity, but then concluded by quoting Rosemary's own words that every garden "'should have a space where you can walk and sit and feel alone with nature . . . a quiet and shady place, with mown paths winding between ornamental trees and shrubs and flowers studding the grass.' Well if you put it like that. . .''

Other obituaries in England included Robin Lane Fox (who called her the Queen of English gardening) writing for the *Financial Times*, Penelope Hobhouse for the *Times*, Mary Keene for the *Daily Telegraph* and *The English Garden*, the editors of *Country Life*, David Wheeler (also writing for *Country Life*), and Joy Larkcom for *The Kitchen Garden*[6]; in America, Anne Raver wrote for the *New York Times* and Tom Fischer for *Horticulture* magazine.

Her passing marked the end of an era. She was very much a product of her generation, with a strong sense of duty, self-discipline, and integrity, along with uncompromising standards in whatever she undertook and an appetite for hard work. Conventional in her values, she was loyal to her family, her village, and her church. Had she been born to a later generation, unconstrained by the strictures of her society and class, she might never have turned to gardening, but with the force of her intelligence and drive, she would probably have succeeded in a profession or even politics. Instead, just when she might have been expected to be winding down and taking things easy, she took up gardening late in life, and despite being a self-taught amateur, became world famous, an inspiring rode model to others.

While she could be critical and demanding, even intimidating, she was hardest on herself. Often she was most severe on those closest to her and could be a tough and exacting boss. That darker edge was softened by her charismatic personality, engaging charm and indefatigable energy. She enjoyed being with people, loved being toasted, and was the life of any party, with her quick laugh and sparkling blue eyes. She was also a generous mentor and promoter of many who had worked for her and a guru to countless others.

Her greatest strength was her ability to communicate. A natural teacher, she was eager to share her hard-earned, hands-on knowledge and skill, along with her infectious enthusiasm. She loved an audience and they loved her; she never talked down to them but always obeyed her own admonition to think about "who is the audience and what is the message?" The message was clear – each person listening to her talk or reading one of her books could and should make beautiful gardens of their own.

Rosemary had arrived on the scene at just the right moment. In the 1980s after the rise of Margaret Thatcher and a long period of Tory government, the English economy finally began to recover from the devastation of the two world wars. In reaction to the loss of cheap gardening labor after the war, the English had turned to ground covers and low-maintenance gardening. The English were ready for formality, beauty, and traditional good taste, ready for Rosemary to re-introduce them to their historic ornamental gardening style.

There was nothing low-maintenance – or what Christopher Lloyd dubbed "low brain-tenance" – about Rosemary's style of gardening. In her view, good gardening meant hard work; the garden was to be watched and managed every day, with careful attention to dead-heading and tidying. With painterly combinations of shrubs, herbaceous plants, and seasonal bulbs and annuals, hers was a high maintenance approach that required careful planning and strict adherence to a schedule of ongoing planting, pruning, lifting, and replanting to keep the garden looking beautiful throughout the year. The potager at Barnsley was particularly influential, demonstrating that a vegetable garden could also be beautiful with a mix of flowers, hedging, and brilliant compositions of the contrasting textures and colors of the vegetables themselves.

The gardens at Barnsley House were relatively small in scale. As a result, her ideas fit easily into large or small spaces and could be easily adapted to both grand and more modestly scaled gardens. Against the handsome backdrop of Barnsley House, her plantings, even though small in scale, were especially photogenic. Thanks to the work of brilliant photographers, such as Jerry Harpur and Andrew Lawson, whose work is reproduced in her many books, her garden ideas and garden designs were disseminated widely.

Drawing upon her library of old herbals and garden writers of earlier centuries, she applied her interest in history and classical gardens to her garden design. Her exuberant plantings were constrained by firm outlines of box hedges and clipped box balls, with the added interest of the height of trees and shrubs shaped into standards. While this seemed obvious, even conventional, by the time she died, it was not in evidence when she began. Rosemary brought beauty and joy back to gardening.

For all her importance in England, Rosemary was a major bridge to America. Unlike many of her countrymen, she admired what she saw in American gardens, endorsing many of them in her books featuring American men and women, and was eager to learn about American plants and ideas. Being so well versed in history, she knew that much of England's plant material had originated there. She frequently traveled to America, usually at least five or six times a year, and was in demand as a garden designer and lecturer there, unequaled by other well-known English gardeners. She especially enjoyed Americans' open friendliness and informality. They enthusiastically returned the affection, and were inspired and encouraged to create their own style of gardening.

By the time she died, gardening styles had begun to shift. Just as the formal gardens of the seventeenth century gave way to the picturesque open landscape of the eighteenth, interest turned to wild meadows and prairie-style planting. Perhaps people began to discover just how much hard work it took to maintain a Rosemary Verey-style flower border, or maybe because she had been copied around the world, they were just ready for something new. Even as other new names arrive on the scene, Rosemary will take her place among the English garden greats, with the likes of William Robinson, Gertrude Jekyll, and Vita Sackville-West.

A traditional funeral service was held on Wednesday June 6, 2001, at St. Mary's Church in Barnsley where Rosemary had served so many years as warden. Prince Charles paid her homage by attending, along with the great and famous of the gardening world, her family, neighbors, and friends. Many of her former gardeners and protégés were also there. Her son Charles gave a short address and her other three children read from scripture. When the vicar was praised for the quality of the service and his remarks, he replied, "I knew I had to get it right, because if I hadn't there would have been a tapping from inside the coffin!"[7]

There was a later memorial service at St. John the Baptist in Cirencester on July 24 with eulogies delivered by Anne Armitage (also known as Anne de Courcy), Simon Verity, Andrew Lawson, and Rosemary's nephew, Paul Sandilands. The 1660 quote from John Evelyn that Rosemary had Simon Verity carve on the plinth at the end of the laburnum walk was quoted on the back cover of the program. "As no man be very miserable that is master of a Garden here; so will no man ever be happy who is not sure of a Garden hereafter. Where the first Adam fell the second rose."

Shortly after the terrible events in New York on September

11, 2001, the New York Botanical Garden also held a memorial tribute for Rosemary. Three years later, an all-day symposium was organized at Cambridge Cottage, Royal Botanic Gardens at Kew on Sunday April 25, 2004. A book of essays and tributes written for the event by fifty-seven friends, admirers, and horticultural greats from England and America was privately published.

Rosemary is buried in the churchyard at Barnsley and shares the same stone with her husband, David.[8] Below the long inscription for him appear her name and the dates of her birth and death, followed by these simple lines:

Mother
OBE VMH
Church Warden
Gardener

Epilogue

You can live on and have influence through words
when all trace of physical reality has vanished.[1]

 T SEEMED inevitable that after Rosemary's death, her son, Charles, would have to sell Barnsley. He tried valiantly to keep the garden going but there simply wasn't enough money. Without Rosemary's star quality and the income earned from her books, her talks, and her garden design work, the revenue from the modest admittance fees for visitors and the sale of plants could not sustain the enterprise. Charles asked the executors of the estate to write on a confidential basis to a small group of friends and knowledgeable leaders in the horticultural world to solicit their advice for the garden's future, including the possibility of a sale. The question put was whether somehow arrangements could be made for the garden, and possibly Rosemary's extensive library, to remain open to the public or, alternatively, to be sold "to a private buyer to do with what he will."

Penelope Hobhouse was one of the recipients of the letter and replied in her usual thoughtful manner. Because the question was so difficult, her reply was full of questions, questions about future leadership, about the need to clear, revive, and edit the garden to avoid having it become "museum-like," asking if the National Trust would take it on while recognizing that a huge endowment would undoubtedly be required. The worst possibility, she felt, would be to have the garden slowly deteriorate. Then she wisely concluded that "Rosemary had an enormous influence on gardening, both here and in America. She was an instinctive educator but although she made her own garden illustrate her ideas the garden may be less important than the impact she had in her lifetime through her books and designs. She will always be remembered for those."[2]

Eventually, Barnsley House was put on the market and sold to Tim Haigh and Rupert Pendered, the two men who owned the village pub. They kept Richard Gatenby on as head gardener and planned to keep the gardens going while they invested heavily in the modification of the house to create an expensive country hotel with a spa added. Barnsley Hotel opened in 2003, but ultimately went into receivership in 2009 as a result of the economic downturn. Another hotel operation bought Barnsley, and so far it continues to operate, although the gardens are certainly not the same. While the basic structures are in place, the intensively planted borders have grown weedy and uninteresting. Rosemary is not there to constantly massage the plantings, ripping out those past their prime and infusing new introductions and ideas. The master's eye is gone.

Although Rosemary was famous for the distinctive garden style she initiated and developed at Barnsley, she was always learning and evolving herself. She continued to experiment with new plants she encountered in other gardens and in the course of her travels. Even pastels were not sacrosanct. When her friend Bob Dash played with bold colors in his own garden at Madoo, she too planted in strong color combinations in one of her borders. She called it her "Bob Dash Border."

Her reaction to the symposium at Kew about the "New Perennials" or the so-called "Dutch" or "German Wave" in 1994 is typical. "Why, I've been doing that for years." If to the eye of beholder it didn't look as though she had been doing that for years, who knows what she might have begun to do had she lived on? Her garden, as her thinking, was never static. Never timid about ripping out an overgrown treasure, she was always a severe editor with a sharp eye and a keen mind open to new ideas that pleased her.

Rosemary was known for a particular flowery style, for her ornamental borders artfully composed of a mix of perennials, annuals, bulbs, trees, and shrubs. She was a superb plantswoman with a genuine gift for creating beautiful plant combinations. Color, texture, and harmonious visuals were her signature. But she recognized, as the garden writer Anna Pavord observed, that the best plants "need a decent frame around them if they are to shine." Anna thought Rosemary's plantings were very English, constrained by "a tight corset and then the absolutely billowing flesh within it." Drawing upon classical garden design and garden history, Rosemary favored formal structures and clear outlines. Her flower borders, profusely planted in a painterly manner and maintained to perfection, were her crowning glory. Within formal outlines, she planted abundantly, in what she called layers, to keep the garden looking lovely in all seasons.

Because her own garden at Barnsley was relatively small, she didn't have a spring border or a separate summer border that was supposed to look good for only one time of year. Instead, all her borders were meant to look wonderful *throughout* the year. Her book, *The Garden in Winter*, emphasized that she meant *all* the seasons. Rosemary continually massaged her borders with great skill and hard work. What she called planting in layers was an approach that required intensive planting and replanting of the same area within other more permanent plants. Spring bulbs would be planted each fall in and among borders of perennials and shrubs, and, once finished, would be lifted out to be replaced by tender annuals. These annuals would later be removed and replaced with yet another planting for fall interest. So the same border would be reworked several times during the growing season to keep it looking good. This approach required constant maintenance and careful planning, both in the design and the propagation needed to keep a constant plant replacement supply at the ready.

Even though her reign as the "Queen of Horticulture" was relatively short – barely twenty years or so – her style became wildly popular and widely imitated, but was rarely matched. Peter Wirtz believes that "she was copied much, but it was never as good as she did it." Peter views her style as highly refined, personal, almost mosaic-like in its blurred flowery mingled drifts, very painterly, but requiring intensive maintenance and therefore quite fragile and vulnerable as a result.

Her moment was a high point in decorative horticulture, creating picturesque and photogenic images, all romantic and blowsy, but beautifully cultivated. To many, she was a great corrective, returning the English to their own garden traditions while validating and supporting Americans developing their own vernacular. With her historical point of reference, she was always attuned to relating the garden to the house, something that did not seem obvious at the time.

Rosemary never claimed to be inventing anything new. Her brilliance was in turning to classical garden design and scaling it down, making it seem possible to achieve. After all, "If she could do something extraordinary, the rest of us could aspire to some success."[3]

Her potager looked to French traditions, but broke new ground in England and America by mixing flowers with vegetables, creating beautiful patterns and growing different vegetables together for their colors and shapes. And it reflected renewed interest in homegrown vegetables. Even the American president has a vegetable garden in the White House these days. As Rosemary urged, why not make vegetable gardens both productive and beautiful? The designer Tom Stuart-Smith was sadly nostalgic in thinking it might no longer be possible for a talented amateur like Rosemary to succeed in the current era's preference for highly credentialed garden designers and landscape architects. He admired Rosemary and thought her potager beautiful but homespun, which made it seem "doable," causing the observer to think "I could build that in a couple of weekends." It is to be hoped that the New York Botanical Garden will eventually implement Rosemary's plans for a potager for others to emulate.

As a result of her success, Rosemary came to personify the English country house style and, like anything that becomes too pervasive, she prompted a reaction. Today, the designs of Piet Oudolph and his followers, with their sweeps of grasses and prairie style, reign supreme just as once Rosemary's garden style did. No doubt in time there will be a shift away from this Dutch-German wave and something else will come along to replace it.

Gardens are ephemeral and garden styles come and go, but Rosemary Verey's most profound message will endure. By example and through her writings, she touched a wide audience, cajoling and finally persuading them that they too could create their own beautiful gardens. After all, she had done it herself so you can do it too. Her spirit and enthusiasm for plants survive in the hearts and gardens of people around the world fortunate to have been touched by her and her message. Her books remain to teach them how, with practical, hands-on advice. But most importantly, her writings continue to carry her lessons and her voice to new generations seeking to create their own gardens. Someone called her the "great encourager." Indeed she was. And I can still hear her proclaiming to all of us, "Just get on with it."

NOTES

CHAPTER ONE

1 *Country Life*, Dec. 17, 1998; Interviews with Victor Norman, Ron Rule, Andrew Lawson.

2 *Remembrances of Rosemary*, written by her family, friends, and colleagues on both sides of the Atlantic, devised by Katherine Lambert for a Rosemary Verey Symposium at Cambridge Cottage, Royal Botanic Garden, Kew, April 25, 2004 (*Kew Remembrances*). Foreword by H.R.H. The Prince of Wales.

3 Rosemary Verey & Barnsley House Garden VHS video produced by Two Four Productions Ltd., in association with *The English Garden*.

4 Desert Island Discs interview of Rosemary Verey, BBC Radio 4, February 13, 1994 ("Desert Island Discs, 1994"). It was a great honor to be featured on this program, part of a radio series. Each program in the series interviews a famous guest who is asked to choose eight pieces of music, along with a book and single item of luxury he or she would take if castaway on a desert island. In the conversation, the guest discusses the reasons for each choice in the context of the guest's life story. The list of those featured is impressive and includes such illustrious names as Sir Kenneth Clark, Joanne Trollope, Archbishop Tutu, Andrew Lloyd Webber, and other famous personages on the world scene of politics and the arts.

5 Interview of Rosemary Verey by Cynthia Lee. *The Guardian*. December 5, 1997. p. 79.

6 Unpublished draft of Rosemary Verey's Autobiography, Chapter One (the "Autobiography").

7 Ibid.

8 Ibid.

9 Simon Verity interview.

10 Ibid.

11 David Verey Diary, February 12 and March 4, 1939.

12 David Verey Diary, May 31, 1939.

13 David Verey Diary, August 6, 1939. On June 6, 1939, the papers printed

a notice of Francis and Gill's engagement. "Mr F. E. P. Sandilands and Miss D. G. Jackson. Francis the younger son of Lieutenant Colonel Prescott Sandilands, DSO, late Royal Marines and Mrs. Sandilands of 121 Coleherne Court and Susan Gillian, youngest daughter of the late Bramwell Jackson, MC and of Mrs. Jackson of Wickham, Newport, Essex."

14 David Verey Diary, August 24, 1939.

15 David Verey Diary, September 15, 1939.

16 Interview of Rosemary Verey in connection with her book, *Rosemary Verey's Good Garden Plans*, by Anne Barrow Clough. "Late Flowering Passion," *Daily Mail*, London, October 26, 1993 (Anne Barrow Clough article).

17 David Verey Diary, September 30, 1939.

18 Lady Sandilands interview.

19 Desert Island Discs, 1994.

20 Anne de Courcy interview.

21 Anne Barrow Clough article.

22 David Verey Diary, October 4, 1939.

23 David Verey Diary, October 21, 1939.

24 Anne Barrow Clough article.

CHAPTER TWO

1 The Autobiography, Chapter One.

2 Desert Island Discs, 1994.

3 Lady Sandilands interview.

4 The Autobiography, Chapter One.

5 Desert Island Discs, 1994.

6 Anne Barrow Clough article.

7 The Autobiography, Chapter One.

8 Pevsner's Buildings of England, a series of architectural guidebooks to the different counties of England begun by Sir Nikolaus Pevsner in the late 1940s, that were later extended to Scotland, Wales, and Ireland. Many of the volumes are still in print, including the two David Verey wrote on Gloucestershire.

9 The Autobiography, Chapter Two.

10 Interview of Rosemary Verey, "The Analyst on Your Couch: A Sin to be Dull," Cynthia Lee, *The Guardian*, December 5, 1997.

11 *James Lees-Milne The Life*, by Michael Bloch (John Murray, 2009).

12 In public remarks at the Garden Museum in November 2010, Sir Roy Strong asserted that Rosemary had a passionate affair with a decorator named David Vicary. Those who knew Vicary believe he was gay, which would be consistent with the many close relationships Rosemary had with gay men later in her life. Vicary seems to have appeared on the scene around 1970. He did some interior decorating for the Vereys and traveled with both of them in England and Europe to visit gardens. Rosemary admired his taste, but after several years the friendship ended. Vicary eventually died a sad and lonely death.

13 Desert Island Discs, 1994.

14 "Gardening Inheritance," by Rosemary Verey, *The Countryman*, Summer, 1968, p. 311.

15 Sir Roy Strong interview.

16 The Autobiography, Chapter Two.

17 Desert Island Discs, 1994.

18 The Autobiography, Chapter Two.

19 Rosemary Verey interview by Pat Blackett, "Health Care Notes: Rosemary Verey," *The Guardian*, September 24, 1996. Rosemary also expressed fear of Alzheimer's saying, "I didn't want to be useless and a nuisance to others."

CHAPTER THREE

1 Simon Verity interview.

2 Rosemary's own adored father also died in 1956. Her mother then left London to move to the village of Burford, very near Barnsley, where she lived with the widow of her late brother. Although Rosemary was influenced by her mother, she rarely talked about her. Her mother died in 1964. Both Rosemary's parents are buried in the church cemetery in Barnsley. According to Gillian Sandilands, her mother often admonished Rosemary, "Don't boss David so much."

3 Rosemary Verey Notes for her unpublished last book ("Notes for Last Book"), in her papers in the possession of Charles Verey (the "Personal Papers.") She observed that Linda's tablet was positioned so that David could see it from their pew and that Linda was "especially still an overpowering influence on D.'s life."

4 The Autobiography, Chapter Two. In Notes for Last Book, she also wrote that for David, hunting had "all become a way of life, rather than a pleasure. David had a horrid time pulling on his hunting boots

and he always wished to go home long before I did. This made me realize I did not want to spend the rest of my life hunting." Before she ceased hunting, it was a major part of her life. Her son Christopher recalled, "Every letter she wrote to me at school told me she had gone hunting and how it had gone."

5 Anne Barrow Clough article.

6 These included Ernest Gimson and the brothers, Ernest and Sidney Barnsley. David Verey's relatives owned one example, Rodmarton Manor, a handsome stone Arts and Crafts house a short drive away from Barnsley. It was designed by Ernest Barnsley and finished in 1929 after twenty years of work. Despite their name, the Barnsley brothers had no relationship to the village of Barnsley where the Vereys lived.

7 Erica Hunningher Interview.

8 The Autobiography, Chapter 3.

9 *Rosemary Verey's Making of a Garden* (1995), p. 133.

10 Rosemary Verey, *The Countryman*, Summer 1969, p. 292.

11 Rosemary Verey Series of Lectures in Australia reported in the *Nationwide News Pty Ltd/Herald*, October 6, 1987.

12 Rosemary Verey, *The Countryman*, Autumn 1968, p. 124–25.

13 Ibid.

14 Rosemary Verey in Peters Perfect Ponds website. "Memories of Barnsley House and Water Garden."

15 The Autobiography, Chapter Three.

16 Letter from Rosemary Verey to Francis Sandilands March 10, 1965. *Kew Remembrances*, Paul Sandilands Essay. p. 8.

17 *Rosemary Verey's Making of a Garden* (1995), p. 100; in the Autobiography, however, she says she went to Bodnant and Powis Castle with Tim Sherrard in the early 1960s.

18 Simon Verity interview.

19 Pevsner's Buildings of England, *Gloucestershire I: The Cotswolds* and *Gloucestershire II: The Vale and Forest of Dean*.

20 Anne Barrow Clough article.

21 "*A Little History of British Gardening*, by Jenny Uglow" reviewed by Sir Roy Strong, *Daily Mail*, April 30, 2004. Uglow mentioned other examples of Rosemary's contemporaries, namely Penelope Hobhouse and Beth Chatto.

Notes

22 Desert Island Discs, 1994.

23 Rosemary Verey, *The Countryman*, Autumn 1971.

CHAPTER FOUR

1 Rosemary Verey, *The Countryman*, Spring 1975, p. 102.

2 *Rosemary Verey's Making of a Garden*, p. 48.

3 Rosemary Verey, *The Countryman*, Spring 1975, p. 103.

4 Caroline Burgess interview. Ms. Burgess is the Executive Director of Stonecrop Gardens, a public garden in Cold Spring, New York, created by Frank and Anne Cabot. After Caroline became Rosemary's full-time gardener, she went off to Kew to study in 1981.

5 Rosemary Verey, *The Countryman*, Spring 1975, p. 103.

6 Anne Barrow Clough article. She also said it would be "awful to go backward. By that, I mean becoming lazier and not always trying to produce the best and letting things slide. I'm seventy-four and it would be a great mistake if I suddenly decided to stay in bed every morning. That would be going backwards, wouldn't it?" Rosemary Verey interview in "Charles: He's a Happy Prince in His Garden" by Steve Whysall, *Vancouver Sun*, February 13, 1993.

7 *Rosemary Verey's Making of a Garden*, p. 93.

8 Notes for Last Book.

9 *Rosemary Verey's Making of a Garden*, pp. 93–94.

10 Rosemary Verey, *The Countryman*, Winter 1972–73.

11 Notes for Last Book.

12 Christopher Verey interview.

13 Ursula Buchan, *Daily Telegraph*, November 18, 2006, saw Rosemary as one of the "greatest and most influential exponents of the potager."

14 Andy Bailey arrived in 1980, Les Bailey a short time later after he finished school. They stayed and were the backbone of the garden until 1995.

15 Rosemary Verey interview, "Feed Your Soil, Advises Author of Books about English Gardening," by Mary Ann Gwinn, *Seattle Times*, February 14, 1993.

16 Veronica Bidwell interview. Focused as he was on the architectural shape of the garden, David at one point did move a well-established yew hedge, which he then clipped into interesting Gothic crenellations, echoing the architecture of the Gothic summerhouse nearby.

Notes

CHAPTER FIVE

1 Simon Verity interview.
2 Rosemary Verey Interview, "Feed Your Soil, Advises Author of Books About English Gardening," by Mary Ann Gwinn, *Seattle Times*, February 14, 1993.
3 Christopher Lloyd letter to Rosemary Verey, November 30, 1979, in Personal Papers.
4 The English edition came out in 1982; the American edition appeared a year later.
5 Ethne Clarke Interview. Penelope Hobhouse was just coming into her own and had been one of the women featured in *The Englishwoman's Garden*. She was first asked to write *The Scented Garden*, but being busy with another book at the time, suggested Rosemary write it instead.
6 Rosemary Verey, *The Scented Garden* (1981), p. 10. This was the first Rosemary Verey book in the author's library, signed by Rosemary Verey at Barnsley House in May of 1983 on the author's first visit there as one of many other visitors.
7 "Gardening Into History," *Daily Telegraph*, November, 1981.
8 Tony Venison, *Country Life*, March 21, 1981.
9 Notebook from January 1975 through August 1977, written after a group of American visitors came to Barnsley House on an Open Day, May 2, 1976, in Personal Papers.
10 Rosemary Verey, *Country Life*. April 30, 1981, p. 1202.
11 *Rosemary Verey's Making of a Garden*, p. 47.
12 Rosemary Verey Diary, January 4, 1982 in Personal Papers.

CHAPTER SIX

1 *Rosemary Verey's Good Planting Plans* (1993), p. 50.
2 *Rosemary Verey's Good Planting Plans* (1993), p. 125.
3 Princess Michael of Kent interview. Princess Michael was born Marie-Christine Anna Agnes Hedwig Ida von Reibnitz and became a member of the British Royal Family when she married Prince Michael of Kent, a grandson of King George V.
4 *Rosemary Verey's Good Planting Plans* (1993), p. 23.
5 *Rosemary Verey's Good Planting Plans* (1993), p. 94.
6 Published in 1983 by New York Graphic Society and reprinted in 1984 by Little, Brown.

Notes

7 The author assisted Ellen Samuels in identifying worthy gardens, writing a short paragraph about her own developing garden for inclusion in the book.

8 *Cotswold Life*, November 1983.

9 Rosemary Verey Diary, October 5, 1983, in Personal Papers.

10 The gravestone reads as follows, with parenthetical explanations added: David Cecil Wynter Verey DL (Deputy Lieutenant of Gloucestershire) FSA (Fellow of the Society of Architects) ARIBA (the Association of the Royal Institute of British Architects) and MA (for his academic degree). 9 September 1913-3 May 1984 Architect Historian Author Captain Royal Fusiliers and S.O.E. High Sheriff of Gloucestershire Chapman Gloucestershire D.A.C. (Diocesan Advisory Committee) Creator Arlington Mill Museum Church Warden of this Parish Lived at Barnsley for forty-five years.

11 Desert Island Discs, 1994.

CHAPTER SEVEN

1 Obituary from local newspaper found in *This Is Our Garden* scrapbook, in Personal Papers.

2 Anne Barrow Clough article.

3 Interview with John Nicholl of Frances Lincoln Limited. His wife, Frances Lincoln, became the principal English publisher of Rosemary Verey's books published after 1987. At this time, Rosemary's five published books were *The Englishwoman's Garden*, *The Englishman's Garden*, *The American Woman's Garden*, *The Scented Garden*, and *Classic Garden Design*.

4 The author was one of them, thanks to a brief paragraph about her garden in the book.

5 Letter to Rosemary Verey from Bob Dash, December, 1985, in Personal Papers. Bob Dash's garden on two acres in Sagaponack is now The Madoo Conservancy, a charitable organization established for its preservation.

6 Rosemary Verey Diary, June 1, 1986, in Personal Papers.

7 Experienced while working at Barnsley by the author, who now stands up straight while clipping her own borders.

Notes

CHAPTER EIGHT

1 Letter from Paul Miles, July 1, 1986, in Personal Papers. Paul goes on in the letter to describe Rosemary as "the honeypot, highly creative and capable of a great deal of original work."

2 David Verey, Will of Record, dated April 29, 1984.

3 The Will also left everything to all four children equally if Rosemary did not survive David or died within twenty-eight days after him.

4 Katherine Lambert interview. Rupert Golby observed she "had a difficult time with the children . . . but there would be a wall put up if she suddenly felt you were getting a bit too close, then the wall would go up. And you wouldn't get any further than that."

5 Penelope Hobhouse interview. Sue Speilberg said that, "Without the garden, not that she would be nothing, but it was the garden that really catapulted her."

6 Renny Reynolds and Jack Staub interview.

7 Lynden Miller interview.

8 Rosemary Verey interview by Cynthia Lee, "The Analyst on Your Couch: It's a Sin to Be Dull," *The Guardian*, December 5, 1997.

9 George Cooper interview, who, like many others, observed she didn't tolerate women as well as she did men.

10 Rosemary Verey, *The Garden in Winter* (1988), p. 7.

11 Ibid., p. 8.

12 Ibid., p. 13.

13 David Wheeler interview.

14 Allen Lacy review, *New York Times*, December 4,1988.

15 Rupert Golby won a gold medal at Chelsea for a garden he created there in 1997, a prize that eluded Rosemary herself.

16 Erica Hunningher interview.

17 Desert Island Discs, 1994.

18 Letter from H.R.H. The Prince of Wales to Rosemary Verey, dated May 22, 1986, in Personal Papers.

19 Desert Island Discs, 1994.

20 *Chicago Tribune*, interview of Rosemary Verey, November 15, 1992.

21 *Rosemary Verey's Good Planting Plans*, p. 6.

22 David Magson interview. The author was seconded to Highgrove for a day while working at Barnsley in 1991. She was assigned to the greenhouse to produce thyme cuttings for the thyme walk. That morning's tedious work resulted in 570 thyme cuttings being potted up.

The thyme walk was the length of a football field, but both Rosemary and Sir Roy Strong warned that the soil for the walk was not conducive to thyme. Ultimately, the entire walk was dug up and the soil reworked to provide the needed sharp drainage, and the thyme walk was replanted again.

23 When the Cottage Garden was being reworked, the gardeners discovered that it had been installed on ground concealing the hidden foundation walls of what had once been a large greenhouse. Not surprisingly, the Cottage Garden failed to thrive.

24 Several years later in 1996, Rosemary was asked to give some business advice to the Duchess of Northumberland about how opening the gardens at Alnwick Castle could be a financial success. She suggested allowing local people to come in for free since they might buy plants and, more importantly, bring visitors who would pay. She also noted that pre-booked tours could be financially rewarding since they would pay for admission and the tour. New York Botanical Garden Library.

CHAPTER NINE

1 *The English Country Garden* (1996), Rosemary Verey accompanies the major television series. p. 22.

2 Plan for Potager Layout of Cooper and Taylor, New York Botanical Garden Library.

3 *The English Country Garden*, p. 22.

4 Desert Island Discs, 1994.

5 Sir Roy Strong interview.

6 Carolyn North interview.

7 Rosemary Verey letter to Robert Key, Estate Manager, December, 1995, New York Botanical Garden Library.

8 Rosemary Verey letter to Robert Key, Estate Manager, August 21, 1996, New York Botanical Garden Library.

9 *The English Country Garden*, p. 71.

10 Ibid., p. 68.

11 *The Sun*, March 14, 1992.

12 Rosemary Verey, *The Flower Arranger's Garden* (1989), p. 9. The Author's copy was signed when she finished working at Barnsley in 1991 and says, "Thank you for all the hard work & tactful selling you have done for four weeks. Rosemary."

13 Rosemary Verey, *The Art of Planting* (1990), p. 7.

Notes

14 Rosemary Verey letter to Paul Martin, February 1991, New York Botanical Garden Library.
15 *The English Country Garden*, p. 28.
16 Elton John turned fifty on March 25, 1997.
17 James Aldridge interview.
18 Carl Neels interview.
19 Rosemary Verey Letter, January 1991, New York Botanical Garden Library.
20 Letter to Ken Bradshaw, December 1992, New York Botanical Garden Library.
21 King Hussein became King at the age of sixteen and died of cancer on February 7, 1999, age sixty-two.
22 Victor Nelson interview.
23 *Rosemary Verey's Good Planting Plans*, p. 59.
24 John Hill interview.

CHAPTER TEN
1 Rosemary Verey Notes, 1991, in Personal Papers.
2 Rosemary Verey, *The American Man's Garden* (1990), Foreword p. vii.
3 Anna Pavord interview.
4 Stephen Lacey interview.
5 Dan Hinkley interview. Dan hopes that "we are over the English border. It doesn't make a lot of sense for our climate and our terroir. You can still see vestiges of it throughout the Northwest but the fever's over. The fever's come and gone."
6 Ron Rule interview.
7 John Nicholl interview.
8 *Kew Remembrances*, Edward Connors essay.
9 Oscar and Annette de la Renta interview.
10 Letter to Rosemary Verey from Oscar de la Renta, June 28, 1993, in Personal Papers.
11 The first edition was printed in 1989 by Gryffon Publications, a private press, followed by a Frances Lincoln edition in 1990; a somewhat later American edition, *A Countrywoman's Year*, appeared in the United States in 1991.
12 *A Countrywoman's Notes* by Rosemary Verey, Foreword by H.R.H. The Prince of Wales.

Notes

13 *Dear Friend & Gardener: Letters on Life and Gardening*, Beth Chatto & Christopher Lloyd (1998).

14 Tom Cooper interview.

15 *Kew Remembrances*, Christopher Lloyd essay.

16 Tom Cooper interview.

17 Joe Eck and Tom Cooper interviews. In Rosemary's view, "The monarchy, like the church, has survived for a great deal of time and everything has its troughs and peaks. I feel quite confident it will survive. I can't visualize England without the Royal Family." "Charles, he's a happy Prince in His Own Garden," Steve Whysall, *Vancouver Sun*, February 13, 1993.

18 Paul Miles interview.

19 Rosemary Verey's handwritten note on a photograph of the event, in Personal Papers.

20 William H. Frederick Jr. interview.

21 Richard and Sheila Sanford interview. They hired Rosemary in 1995.

22 Gregory Long interview.

CHAPTER ELEVEN

1 R.I.B. for Rosemary Isabel Baird. There was no reference to her maiden name of Sandilands. There are many different Royal Orders of Chivalry. The one Rosemary received was among those established by King George V in 1917.

2 "Pictures that Tell a Thousand Plants," Jim Reynolds, *The Irish Times*, November 18, 1995.

3 *Secret Gardens: Revealed by Their Owners* (1995), chosen and edited by Rosemary Verey and Katherine Lambert, p. 11. The author's copy is signed by both after Rosemary wrote in her green ink "For Barbara & Charlie Robinson. I feel so happy that you are 'in' this book! It makes a wonderful contribution & a record of the making of your garden. With love, Rosemary Verey."

4 One later example was on *This Morning*, CBS News, May 19, 1998, where Rosemary was interviewed by Martha Stewart at Kew during the week of the Chelsea Flower Show. Martha Stewart did most of the talking.

5 *The English Country Garden*, Introduction, p. 9. The other gardens featured were Folly Farm (Hon Hugh and Mrs. Astor); Holker Hall

Notes

(Lord and Lady Cavendish); Benington Lordship (Mr. and Mrs. C.H.A. Bott); Kiftsgate Court (Mr. and Mrs. J.G. Chambers); Bledlow Manor (Lord and Lady Carrington); The Grove (Mr. David and Lady Pamela Hicks); Chilcombe House (Mr. and Mrs. J. Hubbard); and Helmingham Hall (Lord and Lady Tollemache). The book is organized into sections following the four seasons.

6 Jane Wykeham-Musgrave interview.

7 Newspaper clipping from unidentified newspaper, in Personal Papers.

8 Nick Burton interview.

9 H. R. H. The Prince of Wales and Charles Clover, *Highgrove: Portrait of an Estate*. 1993.

10 David Magson left Highgrove sometime in 1996 to 1997.

11 Rosemary Verey Obituary, June 2, 2001.

CHAPTER TWELVE

1 Helen Mirren viewed gardening as something that had been very much a royal and aristocratic tradition, particularly the grand schools of landscape design, before it became more democratic in the 1970s. Television helped, but the concept of landscape gardening didn't really become democratized in Britain until the 1980s or 1990s.

2 Letter from Helen Mirren to Rosemary Verey, July 1999, in Personal Papers.

3 Anna Pavord interview, who observed that the Council is made up of "nobs and nabobs."

4 Rosemary Verey Diary, September 17, 1999, in Personal Papers.

5 Anne Norman interview.

6 Rosemary Verey Notes, in Personal Papers.

CHAPTER THIRTEEN

1 *The Englishwoman's Garden* (1980), edited by Alvilde Lees-Milne and Rosemary Verey, p. 143.

2 *Five Centuries of Women and Gardens* by Sue Bennett, (2000), p. 162.

3 The author was the visitor with her husband and was firmly instructed to order a hat from this same milliner for the impending wedding of her son.

4 *Rosemary Verey's Good Planting Plans*, p. 79.

5 *The Economist*, June 16, 2001.

Notes

6 "Remembering Rosemary," Joy Larkcom, *The Kitchen Garden*, October 2001. Rosemary and Joy Larkcom met at the Victoria & Albert Museum in 1978 for an exhibition entitled *The Garden: A Celebration of One Thousand Years of British Gardening*.

7 Jane Wykeham-Musgrave interview.

8 Nearby are David's parents, Constance Lindoraii Verey (1881—1964) and Cecil Verey (1878—1958), along with Linda's sister Violet Emily Birchall, Rosemary's parents, Prescott Sandilands (1878—1956), Lieutenant Colonel Royal Marines, and her mother Gladys Baird Sandilands (1881—1964), as well as her brother, Francis Edwin Prescott Sandilands KT CBE (1913—1995).

EPILOGUE

1 Rosemary Verey notes for her talk on Desert Island Discs, in Personal Papers.

2 Letter from Penelope Hobhouse to William Owen, Dec. 21, 2001.

3 Ursula Buchan, *Daily Telegraph*, November 18, 2006.

ACKNOWLEDGMENTS

I am fortunate in having had the encouragement and support of marvelous people in the writing of this book. Each person who agreed to allow me an interview is named on the list of interviews and each has my deepest gratitude. Whether or not I have quoted them directly, each person provided valuable insights and color to the story.

Special thanks go to Rosemary's four children, Charles Verey, Christopher Verey, Veronica Bidwell, and Davina Wynne-Jones for their help and friendship over the years, a friendship that began long before I thought of writing this book. Not only have I had the pleasure of their company and the privilege of using some of the family's photographs, but Charles and his wife, Denzil, were kind enough to allow me to spend days in their living room poring through boxes of Rosemary's papers, which Charles had carefully organized. Christopher and his wife, Jo, showed me wonderful mementos of Rosemary's early years as a competitive tennis player and shared stories of Rosemary's interest in farming. Veronica and her husband, Robin, made time for me to enjoy the pleasure of their company despite their busy lives, and Veronica, a psychologist by profession, provided important insights into the many individuals involved. Davina herself is now involved in gardening with her own herb business, and always responded generously to my many questions while sharing her own recollections.

Katherine Lambert, Rosemary's long time assistant and the co-editor of one of her books, gave me Rosemary's draft of the first few chapters of an autobiography that never reached fruition, and she helped with other background information I requested too often to recount.

Jerry Harpur and Andrew Lawson, the two brilliant garden photographers whose images helped put Barnsley House gardens on the map, were supportive friends to Rosemary as well as treasured friends of mine, and their photographs are invaluable to this book.

Gregory Long, President of the New York Botanical Garden, Stephen Sinon, the marvelous librarian-archivist, and head librarian Susan Frazier, were generous in allowing me to schedule many days to pore over the boxes of Rosemary's garden designs and related papers that the Library received pursuant to a bequest under her will. The transcripts and tapes of all my interviews will eventually go to the library to be added to their Rosemary Verey archives. I have been fortunate to have been able to use the great resources of the British Library, the New York Public Library, and the library services at my law firm, Debevoise & Plimpton.

First, Dr. Manon Williams and, later, Emily Cherrington, personal secretaries to His Royal Highness The Prince of Wales, were extremely kind and responsive. Dr. Williams arranged for an interview with the Prince, which sadly had to be cancelled at the last moment, but then met with me herself. Emily Cherrington, who also met with me, sent the manuscript to His Royal Highness who thoughtfully provided his corrections to a few of the facts in the chapter about Rosemary's work at Highgrove. Ms. Cherrington obtained his permission for the use of some of Andrew Lawson's photographs of the Cottage Garden at Highgrove and for the reprinting of his tribute to Rosemary in *Kew Remembrances*.

To one of the world's great editors and one of my dearest friends, Kate Medina, I can only say thank you, not only for cheering me on but most importantly, for introducing me to

Acknowledgments

Olga Seham, who became my freelance editor. Olga has been superb, helping me put shape to the story and make intelligent use of the quotes, when I wanted to put in far too many.

Jane Geniesse, who has written several brilliant biographies herself, helped me understand I could set the first scene at any time in the story, and then revert to a chronological approach. And Maria Campbell, a renowned literary agent, offered wise advice along the way, as did Elizabeth Barlow Rogers, founder of the Foundation for Landscape Studies, who has written important books about garden history.

Thanks to the urging of Paula Deitz, I sent a proposal to David R. Godine, who agreed to publish this book even though I had never written a book before. Having taken me on, he also served as my editor and helped me learn to stop writing "like a lawyer!" I have been so fortunate to have David, who cares deeply about publishing, and was the American publisher of Rosemary's second book, *The Englishman's Garden*, turn my manuscript into the kind of beautiful book he is so well known and admired for producing.

Penelope Hobhouse was the first person to read this manuscript in its entirety. She knew Rosemary well and has also been an inspiring role model and friend. Penelope is as important a figure in garden history as Rosemary, and the author of many important books, so her approval has meant the world to me. She also suggested sharing the manuscript with Erica Hunningher, who had served as editor for both Penelope and Rosemary. Erica generously sent me her comments and saved me from making many gaffes as an American when I used slightly wrong words from a British point of view.

My personal assistant, Linda Pehrson, has managed to put my computer copy into proper form with intelligence, skill, and unflagging cheer, sending the manuscript instantly to London, Boston, and New York both by email and in hard copy on very short notice, making it all look easy when it wasn't.

There never would have been a story to tell had it not been for my close friend, Penny Bardel, without whom I never would have had a house in Washington, Connecticut, in which to learn to garden, nor learned to love English gardens through my early visits with her when she lived there. It was Penny who suggested I go work in a great garden, rather than try to find a suitable course of horticultural study during my sabbatical from my law firm. That, of course, is how I came to work at Barnsley House for Rosemary Verey who became my boss and ultimately my very special friend.

But the most important person in all of this, as in everything in my life, is my extraordinary husband and love of my life, Charlie. Very much like the story of Rosemary and David's gardening partnership, Charlie enticed me into my first gardening efforts and then went on to shape the landscape, offering me new canvases to paint with plants. The many original structures that make our gardens at Brush Hill so distinctive are his designs and hand-built creations. Not only did he put up with my leaving him behind when I left to work at Barnsley, he too became a big fan of Rosemary's and knew I could write this book. Then he kept my feet to the fire – or rather, my bottom glued to the chair in front of my computer – pressing me, just as Rosemary did, to just get on with it.

SELECTED BIBLIOGRAPHY

Sue Bennett, *Five Centuries of Women & Gardens*, National Portrait Gallery Publications (2000).

Richard Bisgrove, *William Robinson: The Wild Gardener*, Frances Lincoln (2008).

Michael Bloch, *James Lees-Milne: The Life*, John Murray (2009).

Ursula Buchan, with Anna Pavord and Brent Elliott, *Garden People: The Photographs of Valerie Finnis*, Thames & Hudson (2007).

Anne de Courcy, *Debs At War, 1939–1945: How Wartime Changed Their Lives*, Weidenfeld & Nicolson (2005).

HRH The Prince of Wales and Charles Clover, *Highgrove: Portrait of an Estate*, Chapmans (1993).

Penelope Hobhouse, *The Story of Gardening*, Dorling Kindersley (2002).

The Illustrated Virago Book of Women Gardeners, edited by Deborah Kellaway, Virago Press (1995).

Christopher Lloyd and Beth Chatto, *Dear Friend and Gardener*, Frances Lincoln (1998).

Arthur Marwick, *British Society Since 1945*, Penguin Books Ltd. (1982).

Arthur Marwick, *The Sixties: Cultural Revolution in Britain, France, Italy, and the United States, c. 1958–1974*, Oxford University Press (1998).

Russell Page, *The Education of a Gardener*, William Collins Sons & Co. (1962).

Elizabeth Barlow Rogers, *Landscape Design: A Cultural and Architectural History*, Harry N. Abrams, Inc. (2001).

Jenny Uglow, *A Little History of British Gardening*, Chatto & Windus (2004).

David Verey, *Cotswold Churches*, B.T. Batsford (1976).

Twigs Way, *A Nation of Gardeners*, Prion (2010).

PEOPLE INTERVIEWED

James Aldridge 10-19-06
Anne De Courcy Armitage 11-01-07
Antony Beck 6-9-08
Lizinka M. Benton 4-9-07
Simon Biddulph 4-4-07
Veronica Bidwell 10-18-06
Felicity Bryan 11-29-06
Caroline Burgess 3-9-07
Nick Burton 4-3-07
Frank Cabot 12-06-06
Anne Cox Chambers 8-29-07
Jo Christian 10-10-08
Ethne Clarke 1-20-10
Thomas C. Cooper 12-3-07
George Cooper 3-12-08
Bob Dash 3-7-07
Oscar and Annette de la Renta 11-15-08
Joe Eck 4-2-08
David Farquharson 4-03-06
William H. Frederick, Jr. 3-15-06
Ryan Gainey 8-8-07
Richard Gatenby 4-6-09
Rupert Golby 10-17-06
Deborah Goodenough 6-11-10
Jerry Harpur 10-19-06
John Hill 5-17-06
Dan Hinkley 6-2-08
Penelope Hobhouse 4- 2-07
David Howard 1-23-08
Marguerite Hoffnung 10-16-06
Erica Hunningher 10-20-06
Stephen Lacey 10-20-06

People Interviewed

Katherine Lambert 5-16-06
Gregory Long 6-22-06
Andrew Lawson 5-17-06
David Magson 2-19-08
Princess Michael of Kent 10-15-08
Paul Miles 6-27-08
Lynden B. Miller 1-30-07
Helen Mirren 8-05-08
Carl Neels 2-13-08
Victor Nelson 4-07-06
John Nichol 10-10-08
Victor and Anne Norman 4-05-09
Carolyn North 4-3-07
Serge Pauleau 8-29-07
Anna Pavord 11-30-09
Rupert Pendered 4-6-09
Tim Rees 10-19-06
Arthur S. Reynolds 2-13-07
Renny Reynolds and Jack Staub 8-29-09
Ron Rule 3-15-08
Lady Salisbury 2-19-08
Richard and Sheila Sanford 9-15-07
Gillian Sandilands 2-06 and 4-1-07
Sue Spielberg 4-4-07
Sir Roy Strong 10-16-06
Thomas Stuart-Smith 2-8-10
Jean Sturgis 10–12-08
Marco Polo Stufano 2-7-07
Kim Tripp 6-12-07
Christopher and Jo Verey 5-18-06
Charles Verey 5-18-06
Simon Verity 3-27-06
David Wheeler 8-28-08
Hon. Hilary Weston 7-27-2010
Peter Wirtz 10-5-10
Jane Wykeham-Musgrave 4-3-09
Davina Wynne-Jones 10-17-06

BOOKS BY ROSEMARY VEREY

The Englishwoman's Garden (1980)
Edited by Alvilde Lees-Milne and Rosemary Verey
Chatto & Windus (UK)

The Herb Growing Book (1980)
Walker Books (UK)
Little, Brown (US)

The Scented Garden (1981)
Michael Joseph (UK)
Alfred A. Knopf (US)

The Englishman's Garden (1982)
Edited by Alvilde Lees-Milne and Rosemary Verey
Allen Lane, Penguin Books (UK)
David R. Godine (US) (1983)

The American Woman's Garden (1984)
Rosemary Verey and Ellen Samuels
New York Graphic Society / Little, Brown (US)

Classic Garden Design (1984)
Viking/Penguin Books (UK)
Congdon & Weed, Random House (US)

The New Englishwoman's Garden (1987)
Edited by Alvilde Lees-Milne and Rosemary Verey
Chatto & Windus (UK)
Salem House (US) (1988)

The Garden in Winter (1988)
Frances Lincoln Windward (UK)
New York Graphic Society / Little, Brown (US)

Books by Rosemary Verey

The Flower Arranger's Garden (1989)
Conran Octopus (UK)
Little, Brown (US)

Good Planting (1990)
Frances Lincoln (UK)

The Art of Planting (1990)
Little, Brown (US)

The American Man's Garden (1990)
Little, Brown (US)

The Garden Gate (1991)
Pavilion Books (UK)
Simon & Schuster (US)

A Countrywoman's Notes (1991)
Frances Lincoln (UK)
Little, Brown (US) (as *A Countrywoman's Year*)

A Gardener's Book of Days (1992)
Frances Lincoln (UK)
Little, Brown (US)

Rosemary Verey's Good Planting Plans (1993)
Frances Lincoln (UK)
Little, Brown (US)

Secret Gardens: Revealed by Their Owners (1994)
Chosen and edited by Rosemary Verey and Katherine Lambert
Ebury Press, Random House (UK)
Little, Brown (US)

Rosemary Verey's Making of a Garden (1995)
Frances Lincoln (UK)
Henry Holt (US)

The English Country Garden (1996)
BBC Books (UK)

INDEX

239

Index

Index

Index

Index

Index

Index

Index

Index

Index

PHOTOGRAPH CREDITS

Photographs following p. 28:

H. R. H. The Prince of Wales and Rosemary Verey on page 1, courtesy of *Country Life*.
Rosemary in the Laburnum Walk on page 1 by Andrew Lawson.
Photographs on pages 2, 3, and 4 are courtesy of the Verey family.

Photographs following p. 76:

Barnsley House with rock roses on page 1 by Andrew Lawson.
The Gothick Summer House on page 1 by Jerry Harpur.
The Temple on page 1 by Andrew Lawson.
The Winter Walk and the Laburnum Walk on page 2 by Andrew Lawson.
Barnsley House with red poppies on page 2 by Jerry Harpur.
The Knot Garden in front of the verandah on page 3 by Jerry Harpur.
The Knot Garden in frost and the Herb Garden on page 3 by Andrew Lawson.
Planting patterns in the Potager on page 4 by Andrew Lawson.
Arches in the Potager on page 4 by Andrew Lawson.

Photographs following p. 124:

The frog fountain and statue of the hunting lady on page 1 by Andrew Lawson.
Holdenby House and Little House on page 2 by Andrew Lawson.
Fort Belvedere and Rosemary's model garden on page 3 by Andrew Lawson.
Rosemary in the conservatory on page 4 by Jerry Harpur.
Tools in the potting shed on page 4 by the author.
Rosemary with Andrew Lawson and Jerry Harpur on page 4 by Briony Lawson.

Photograph Credits

Photographs following p. 172:

H.R.H. The Prince of Wales and Rosemary at Highgrove and the Cottage Garden on page 1 by Andrew Lawson.
Sir Elton John and David Furnish on page 2, courtesy of Press Association Images.
The scented garden and rill at Woodside on page 2 by Andrew Lawson.
Rosemary with the Japanese delegation and Rosemary with Christopher Lloyd on page 3 by the author.
Rosemary with the author on page 3 by Charles Raskob Robinson.
Rosemary with Irish cap on page 4 by the author.
Richard and Sheila Sanford's garden on page 4 by Sheila Sanford.
Antony and Angela Beck's garden on page 4 by Pieter Estersohn.

On the endpapers:

Plan of Barnsley House & Garden, courtesy of Charles Verey.

DESIGN & COMPOSITION BY CARL W. SCARBROUGH